THE INFINITE BONDS OF FAMILY:
DOMESTICITY IN CANADA, 1850–1940

The history of the family is a relatively new, yet rapidly developing area of academic study. With this book, Cynthia Comacchio presents the first historical overview of domestic life in Canada.

According to Comacchio, the social anxiety resulting from an ongoing perception of the family as being 'in crisis' has had a significant influence on evolving social policy. Comacchio shows how families have both changed and remained the same through transitions brought about by urbanization, industrialization, and war. Her many stories of individual families highlight both historical trends and the more intimate issues related to race, gender, class, religion, and age.

This is the only synthesis to date of the historical literature on Canadian families. Designed for students at graduate and undergraduate levels, it not only introduces the key concepts and approaches of a developing field of study, but also summarizes the major issues and trends that affected Canadian families from 1850 to 1940.

CYNTHIA R. COMACCHIO is an associate professor of history and women's studies at Wilfrid Laurier University.

THEMES IN CANADIAN HISTORY

Editors: Craig Heron and Colin Coates

CYNTHIA R. COMACCHIO

The Infinite
Bonds of Family:
Domesticity in Canada,
1850–1940

UNIVERSITY OF TORONTO PRESS
Toronto Buffalo London

© University of Toronto Press Incorporated 1999
Toronto Buffalo London

Printed in Canada
ISBN 0-8020-0964-6 (cloth)
ISBN 0-8020-7929-6 (paper)

Printed on acid-free paper

Canadian Cataloguing in Publication Data

Comacchio, Cynthia R., 1957–
 The infinite bonds of family : domesticity in Canada, 1850–1940

(Themes in Canadian social history)
Includes bibliographical references and index.
ISBN 0-8020-0964-6 (bound)   ISBN 0-8020-7929-6 (pbk.)

1. Family – Canada – History. I. Title. II. Series.

HQ559.C65 1999   306.85'0971   C99-930128-4

University of Toronto Press acknowledges the financial
assistance to its publishing program of the Canada Council
for the Arts and the Ontario Arts Council.

Contents

Acknowledgments

For their counsel and encouragement, I thank my colleagues Suzanne Zeller and Sandra Woolfrey, Wilfrid Laurier University; Denyse Baillargeon, Université de Montréal; André Turmel, Université de Laval; Neil Sutherland, University of British Columbia; J.R. Miller, University of Saskatchewan; Jeff Taylor, Athabasca University; and Chad Gaffield, University of Ottawa. For their editorial support and assistance, thanks are also due to the University of Toronto Press: in particular to Craig Heron, Franca Iacovetta, Gerry Hallowell, and Emily Andrew.

While putting together this little book, I was constantly aware of the ways in which home, work, and family intersect. For inspiration and sustenance, I have looked to my children, Stefanie and Evan; my parents, Bruno and Maria Comacchio; my siblings, John and Lorna Comacchio, and Linda and Murray Calanchie; my nieces, Blaire and Brenna Comacchio; and my (very) extended family on the Canadian side: thirteen aunts/uncles, twenty-seven first cousins, and a newly arrived generation of five second cousins.

For getting all this started, I dedicate this book to the fond memory of my grandparents, Maria Favrin and Giovanni Comacchio, and Maria Rech and Fiorino Fillipetto. Their own family histories span old world and new, and the better part of the years considered here.

CYNTHIA R. COMACCHIO
GUELPH, ONTARIO

THE INFINITE BONDS OF FAMILY:
DOMESTICITY IN CANADA, 1850–1940

Introduction:
Thinking Historically about
Canadian Families

In a hurried few pages, a young man newly arrived in Canada in the early years of the twentieth century wrote to his mother in Italy. Sketching some details about his life and work here, he closed with a filial declaration that, with variations in phrasing, must have comforted many a faraway family: 'Only God can know when we will see each other again, but the infinite bonds of family keep you and my brothers and sisters always with me.' Across the distance, his mother and siblings undoubtedly understood the love, longing, and sense of duty embodied in those bonds.

By drawing out pertinent connections between the history of families in Canada and our wider national history, this book outlines some of the ways in which 'the infinite bonds of family' have constituted themselves over the course of a near-century. To this end, I have borrowed from the published work of historians and historical sociologists who have studied Canadian family history and its many related topics for the years between 1850 and 1940. This 'nation-building' period witnessed Confederation, westward expansion, the subjugation of Native peoples, industrialization, a 'war to end all wars,' women's suffrage, and the worst economic depression of this century – to select but a few of its pivotal moments.

Where the history of families is concerned, if there is one thread that winds unbroken through this era of rapid and intensive change, it is a widespread public perception that 'the family' was in a state of crisis. The nature of the crisis, its intensity, and the solutions proposed, all changed in relation to the pressing 'problems' of the day. What remained constant, at least among middle-class Euro-Canadian commentators, was a conviction that the crisis was ongoing. Clearly, this perception involved a popular understanding of 'crisis' that contradicts the term's true meaning. At every turn, however, those fretting about 'the Canadian family' also grasped the sense of opportunity that 'crisis' conveyed. They were committed to the comforting ideal of a particular family model that could withstand any demon and carry the nation to its own best destiny. The logical corollary was that certain social groups were qualified to define this ideal, to identify as 'deviant' the families that did not meet it, and to decide how best to assist those deviant families in coming up to expectations.

History shows us the futility of trying to speak of 'the family.' Most human beings have spent at least some part of their lives with their families of origin, or in family settings modelled on them. Despite their universal qualities, there are also many identifiable forms of family in any culture, in any historical moment. For all the continuities through time, it is evident that families also change, both over the life course of their members, and over the course of history. Families live out histories of their own while also participating actively in the larger arena of national history. There is, ultimately, very little historical space that 'family' does not impinge upon.

The relationships of family and society are so interconnected that change can emanate from either source. It is often difficult to tell whether families are acting as agents of change or as its recipients. To describe the experiences of Canadian families during these eventful years, I have juxtaposed pervasive ideals about 'the family' with what we know about the material, day-to-day realities of family life. To date, family historians are much clearer on ideas about 'the family' than about the actual details of family life – the everyday family cultures defined by ordinary people. The overview contained in these pages naturally reflects that tendency in the literature.

The variables that make 'family' at once unique and universal – class, gender, region, race, ethnicity, religion, and age, among the most important – are also considered throughout this book. These identifying concepts and relations shape, and are shaped by, bonds that are infinite in nature and scope. Even when they are disturbed, by immigration, for example, or the removal or departure of children or spouses – or severed by abandonment, death, divorce – familial bonds are never effectively destroyed. Elastic with possibilities, they are the basis of our individual histories. Families have been, and always will be, at once supportive and restrictive, nurturing and oppressive, protective and abusive, innovative and conservative, liberating and entrapping. As the historical literature indicates, families persist because they are elemental, and change because they are constructed and reconstructed to meet specific social needs and objectives.

We could effectively borrow a concept from the biological sciences – 'punctuated equilibrium'– to chart the historical paths of Canadian families over this period. Such a 'family time-line' would show a fairly steady course, marking the persistence of families through history. But we would also see sharp points of disruption, the process gradually evening out again as these 'jolts' were met by adaptation and restabilization. By envisioning families acting historically in this manner, we can trace hold-overs or continuities from 'traditional' families, as well as the 'breaks' that are reflected in new family models, or what contemporaries recognized as 'modern' families.

Perhaps most potent of all are the metaphorical meanings of family. Premised on the power and leadership of men as fathers/rulers, and on the reproductive role of women – the basis of the social organization known by the familial term 'patriarchy'– social and political structures reflect and reinforce family structures. There was much overlap between Protestant religious and political discourses in Upper Canada before Confederation, for example. Both affirmed 'paternal' rule and 'separate spheres' for women and men. The governing 'Family Compact' in Upper Canada and its equivalent,

the 'Château Clique' in Lower Canada, actually comprised
elite networks sustained by marriage, family, and kinship ties.
Particularly strong in Quebec in this time, the Roman Catholic Church sanctified the cult of the Holy Family, especially
that of Mary, Mother of God, and made the Pope – the Holy
Father – head of the Family of Man. Labour and socialist
organizations also borrowed the language of family to stress
the bonds of class solidarity, as did the many 'fraternal' associations of the nineteenth century. Women formed organizations bound by 'sisterhood' and motivated by a reform
impulse defined in maternal terms.

Much of the family's symbolic power comes from the religious, moral, and ideological forces that have sustained it in
the face of continued threats, real and imagined. Add to these
the power of the law, education, science, and the state, and
it is clear why the family's institutional basis is so durable. A
pervasive ideology of 'familism' has left few social relations
untouched. 'The family' is not only a product of the larger
society, therefore, but also its producer and reproducer. Any
adequate historical understanding of family must acknowledge its central role in social and political as well as personal
relationships, in societal as well as biological reproduction.
'The family' may be classified as a 'natural' or biological unit,
a 'traditional,' divinely ordained, and universal entity, but it
is also very much a social construction. It is whatever we need
it to be, at once the source of all good and of all evil.

Given the countless and varied meanings that 'family' carries, finding a way to approach families historically is a complicated exercise. Historians have adopted some of the concepts
and methods of the social sciences to conceptualize and
contextualize studies of families in the past. Social scientists
use the term 'family' to describe a kinship and legal unit
based on relationships of marriage or biology (parent–child
linkages). 'Household' refers to a residential unit and to both
kin and non-kin who share that common residence. The
'nuclear' or 'conjugal' family is composed of a husband, wife,
and their dependent children, living in an independent house-

hold. 'Extended families' are usually multigenerational, include kin related by blood as well as by marriage. Eve we use such definitions, we have to be mindful that most people define 'family' subjectively, according to their own perspectives and experiences, and the historical forces that have shaped them. Social groups also vary in conceptualizing 'family.' Some Native Canadians stressed descent through the paternal or maternal line; others gave more weight to horizontal ties of kinship, as acquired through marriage, than to these vertical ones. In most cases, however, Aboriginal definitions of family extended well beyond the household, as work, trade, and political relations were organized through kin networks. Immigrant and African-Canadian family groupings have also been more likely to be multigenerational than those of Anglo-Celtic 'Canadians,' in keeping with both cultural practices and material necessities.

Historians' interest in families awakened in the 1960s with the emergence of the 'new social history,' which aimed to uncover the lives of the inarticulate majority who had left few traditional records. Demographic historians used statistics from census schedules, parish records, and government and legal documents to examine patterns of family life such as residence, household size, organizational structure, kinship networks, age relations, developmental cycles, inheritance systems, and migration. For these historians, the decisive shifts in family history over the past 200 years have been structural. The demographic approach has greatly expanded our knowledge about such important trends as declining family size and mortality rates, increasing childhood dependence, and the timing of life-stages. But it cannot convey much sense of the emotional, qualitative textures of everyday domestic relations, or of the internal power dynamics of families. Its focus on families as units begged an understanding of the lives of their individual members, and members' interactions both among themselves and with outside institutions.

Building on demographic findings, a second group of family historians developed a more dynamic, relational approach by studying the life-course of families. Life-course historians are concerned with the relationship between the life-stages of individual family members and the larger family cycle. Family decisions and actions are viewed as adaptations to the changing ages and roles of members, and also to external social, economic, and political pressures. The 'family strategies' approach is frequently used in combination with life-course analysis. It considers how families earn their subsistence, acquire property, transmit land, sustain and improve living standards, strengthen and preserve kinship ties, educate children. Late-nineteenth-century families enduring economic insecurity might temporarily remove children from school and send them to work, or take in boarders, for example. It is also likely that these families enjoyed their highest standard of living when older children were still living at home and contributing wages to the family economy.

A third approach to the history of families, sometimes called the 'sentiments' or 'emotions' approach, is perhaps methodologically closer to the history of ideas than to the social sciences. Focusing on sociocultural values, expectations, images, and roles assigned to 'the family,' its practitioners pay attention to such things as courtship, childrearing, sexual conduct, marriage practices, literary images, gender constructions, and public discourses. Using qualitative more than quantitative evidence, they aim to reconstruct the complex and often contradictory aspects of family life, and to integrate the study of individuals and families with the broader sociocultural phenomena grounding their experiences. We can then see that age differentiation – the experiences of childhood, adolescence, adulthood, old age – results as much from historically specific social meanings ascribed to those life-stages as from the biological facts of birth, sexual maturity, and death. In this way, we learn that 'childhood' was a privilege extended only to the middle and upper classes until the early years of the twentieth century, and that what we know as 'adolescence' was even slower to become a universal experience among teenagers.

The identifying marks inscribed by class, race, ethnicity, region, and religion are also crucial to understanding both the variety of family forms and relations at any given moment, and prevailing ideals about family. Just as they differentiate family experiences, they serve to distinguish the 'norm.' In English Canada, families have been measured against a white, middle-class, Anglo-Celtic, Protestant, central Canadian standard. In Quebec, the strength of the Catholic Church throughout this period has been instrumental in promoting a certain family model depicting large, devout, rural families as the key to cultural and religious survival in a materialistic North America. Despite the obvious religious and cultural differences, there are many similarities between these two models. They both support masculine authority, feminine submission, and the reproduction of certain socially defined qualities. They are clearly hierarchical, and they clearly define those who, because of race, religion, or 'deviance,' do not fit the approved model.

Because definitions of femininity and masculinity are centred on familial roles, gender analysis has proven to be an effective method for approaching such ideals critically. Feminist historians have demonstrated that the declining birth rate, the emergence of motherhood as a self-conscious vocation, the growing labour-force participation of women, and the upward trend in divorce are familial trends closely entwined with women's changing socio-economic status. New interest in the social construction of masculinity has also led historians to question assumptions about male domestic roles, and how these 'fit' with larger patriarchal structures and the public status ascribed to 'breadwinning.' State formation and social reproduction are related issues that concern family historians. 'The family' is not only the main location of biologically and legally defined relationships between men and women, adults and children, but also where private and public spheres intersect. It is the socially and legally sanctioned site both for biological reproduction and for the care and socialization of family members: the social reproduction which has historically been women's work. In this sense, in regards to both wage labour and the usually unpaid feminine domestic labour, the work of families is to sustain a certain kind of society. Families replicate values and belief systems, forging the links between personal identity and social role, individuals and society, home and nation. During the twentieth century, the state has increasingly supported their efforts towards these ends.

Because of the kinds of questions and sources that family history involves, and the interwoven, overlapping nature of its subjects and areas, some combination of perspectives and approaches is generally required. Many of the studies currently available in the expanding field of Canadian family history fit comfortably within more than one classification, as the brief select bibliographies included in this book will testify. Despite the obvious wealth of approaches and the growing historiography, it is also evident that many gaps remain. We still know few details about Aboriginal families in this period, particularly about daily domestic life on the reserves. We know little about Inuit families, African-Canadian families, single-parent families. Domestic violence and incest, sex education and sexual relations, homosexuality and lesbianism, are topics just opening up to historical research. Motherhood is relatively well covered, fatherhood scarcely at all, and there is still much to be learned about birth control in Canada. We have few analyses of the culture of adolescence. We are only beginning to probe the sociocultural contours of an ageing society. The relationship among ideals about family, actual families, and the evolution of the welfare state needs further study. And, just as we seem to know more about family ideals than family realities, we also seem to know more about the unhappy aspects of family life than about its positive elements. Such unhappy experiences are probably more likely to be captured in historical records than are the daily contentedness and emotional security that are also fundamental components of family histories.

As the twenty-first century nears, there is obviously much

work for family historians to do. The brief overview offered in these pages suggests just how rich a literature on family is now available to us. I hope that it may also point students of Canadian history in fruitful directions that will eventually narrow the historiographical gaps. Our family histories are something individual to all of us, but they are also something we have in common. Together, they constitute a vital part of our collective memory, and therefore our national history.

PART I
MAKING THE NEW NATION:
DOMESTIC ADJUSTMENTS, 1850–1914

1

The New Order: Socio-economic Changes and Family Relations

Between the second half of the nineteenth century and the outbreak of the First World War in 1914, a new nation was created and set on a dynamic developmental path. A predominantly family-based agrarian economy, in which men, women, and children all played distinct but interdependent productive roles, shifted into one featuring mechanized, male-dominated production. Industry grew and cities expanded as the labour market responded to rural out-migration and immigration from overseas. By 1900, there were 70,000 factories in Canada; 60 per cent of the labour force was non-agricultural. During the so-called second industrial revolution commencing with the new century, hundreds of smaller industrial concerns merged into the large corporations characteristic of modern capitalism. Workers organized for their own protection. Women clamoured for, and expanded, their access to education, employment, and public participation. Childhood slowly became a time of schooling rather than work. Adolescence became a more distinctive life-stage. The always-tenuous position of the elderly came to be seen as another of the new age's many social problems. The intensive pace and nature of change, and the many challenges to social order that ensued, also gave rise to an organized response in the Social Gospel, the largest movement of activist Christianity ever known in Canada.

This chapter considers the relationship of structural and

familial change during these tumultuous years, focusing on the larger trends as they affected families and their individual members. In the transfer from countryside to city, from Europe and Asia to crowded urban centres and isolated prairie homesteads, from family-based production and small business to factory production and corporate employment, families met the challenge of regaining a certain balance in the midst of rapid change. Here is our first recognizable moment of 'punctuated equilibrium.'

Setting the Stage: Families in Colonial Times

When Europeans 'discovered' the North American continent, they found not empty territory, but vast expanses inhabited by Aboriginal peoples whose social, political, and economic organization was a complex network based on kinship. These early Native cultures differed widely in their notions of kinship, but they all subsumed the nuclear family in a larger system of kin and marital alliances. Intricate ties of blood and ceremonial kinship organized rights and obligations in all aspects of life: naming a child at birth, residence, labour, trade, gender relations, political and cultural leadership, diplomacy and war, marriage and divorce, death and inheritance. The network was extended as widely as possible, through rituals of kinship reciprocity and ceremonial friendships, games and hospitality. In contrast, the system preferred by Europeans allotted property and inheritance rights to separate families in separate households, thereby distinguishing them from each other through social and economic status. This system was part of a larger mode of production that, once in place in the North American colonies, would find Aboriginal principles of social organization 'uncivilized,' and an obstacle to European dominance. Protestant and Catholic missionary efforts, sustained by imperial and colonial governments, tried to replace Aboriginal customs of family life and social reproduction with their own. Some First Nations peoples managed to maintain some of their traditions,

but many were undermined, even virtually oblite
clash between the two.

From the beginnings of European interest ...
World,' families were crucial to plans formulated in impe.
centres of power. Marriages and families, more than military
might or mercantile trade, would claim this land from the
wilderness and from its Aboriginal inhabitants. The fur trade
that dominated the early socio-economic history of North
America is chiefly regarded as the endeavour of individual
(male) adventurers or organizations such as the Hudson's
Bay or North West companies. But this popular image ignores
the fundamental role that families played in the conduct and
success of these ventures, and slights the cross-cultural impact of different notions of 'family.' The taking of Aboriginal 'country wives' was common among traders and officers
of both companies. Native people sought to strengthen trade
relations with kinship ties, as was their custom, and the traders benefited from the active assistance, companionship, and
domestic labour that Native wives ably provided. Much of the
labour force of the fur-trade companies consisted of the
children of these marriages, the first generations of the Métis
people instrumental in the creation of Manitoba in 1870.

In the frontier colonies of British North America, marriage
was at once a civic duty and an individual imperative. Without well-established systems to police the population and to
provide for its needy members, colonial society depended on
stable families to guard against disorder and lawlessness. The
vast majority of the settler population lived on farms and
engaged in some combination of agriculture and fishing,
lumbering, or the fur trade. Material security could be attained only through collective labour – the labour of family
members working as one person, in a 'one for all' capacity.
Men concentrated on land clearing, the principal crops, and
the husbandry of large animals. Women and children took
charge of domestic production, weaving fabrics which were
made into the family's clothing, knitting, rug-braiding, plant-
ing vegetables, and raising chickens and other small animals.

The household tasks of cooking, cleaning, and childcare were performed by mothers and daughters, who were trained in these 'feminine' skills from a very early age.

By mid-century, industrial development was accompanying U.S. and British demand for Canadian grain and lumber and the corresponding expansion of agriculture. Although handicraft production still predominated in the 1850s, 'manufactories' were bringing together various craftsmen into one operation. Many of these early industrial concerns were new or expanding family businesses. In some sectors, such as textiles, domestic activity was still a significant part of the production process, as households began producing cloth and yarn for sale to dressmakers and weavers. Nonetheless, the productive aspects of domestic labour – much of it traditionally performed by unpaid women and children – were gradually moving into the marketplace. Opportunities for unskilled and semi-skilled wage labour grew. With workers and work leaving the household, the family economy was increasingly integrated with the emerging cash economy. Wage labour became part of the life-course of unmarried young people, allowing them to contribute to the family economy, and eventually to leave their parents' homes and set up on their own.

The predominant family form in nineteenth-century British North America was nuclear, with one 'conjugal unit'– man, woman, and their children – per separate household. At various times, depending on the family's fortunes and life-course, as well as those of kin and neighbours, the household might absorb extra members. Often these were live-in domestic servants or agricultural labourers, or, as was customary in the preindustrial trades, boarded apprentices. These servants and apprentices were frequently kin, or the children of close friends, in keeping with the tradition of 'sending out' adolescent children to other families for training and socialization, a practice much on the wane after mid-century. All children were cherished as part of the collectivity in traditional Aboriginal cultures, and orphans were readily adopted, often into related families. Among the Inuit, it was believed that the best marriages involved a brother/sister exchange between two sets of cousins: a brother and sister of one family would marry a sister and brother of another, building layers of kin relations upon each other, a condition known as 'tamalrutit.' In African-Canadian communities, group solidarity and cooperation for the common good were also sustained by an expansive sense of family. Between 1851 and 1857, the passengers on Harriet Tubman's Underground Railroad trips to southwestern Ontario were often the relatives of African Canadians who asked her to conduct their families out of slavery. Young refugees were absorbed into new family groupings.

The presence of additional household members depended also on the specific stage of a family's life-course. Elderly grandparents, especially widows, might join the household when they could no longer cope independently. Families with young children might take in paying boarders at that expensive life-stage, also a common strategy for families headed by widowed or deserted women. High mortality, especially among women in childbirth, and the economic necessity of reconstituting the family unit, encouraged high rates of re-marriage and the blending of families from previous marriages. Even for nineteenth-century Canadians living in nuclear families, the idea of family was necessarily expansive because kinship support systems were vital to survival. In view of scant public provision for health and welfare, and grudging organized charity, kin could be counted on for assistance with illness, childbirth, untimely deaths, and personal and financial stresses of all kinds. Few could live and prosper outside families.

Cultural Change and Family Values: The Cult of Domesticity

The material conditions of colonial life played a significant role in shaping families, but so did ideas about the well-ordered polity and its social relations. British North America was a hierarchical society with clear distinctions between the colonial elite and the lower ranks. Classified by their 'race,' Aboriginal people, Black Loyalists and refugee slaves, and the 'famine Irish' were reserved the lowest ranks. The social structure was also intensely patriarchal, based upon the 'natural' rule of men as 'governors' of state, economy, and family. Women could not participate in the political process, higher education, the professions, or the higher realms of commerce. Men controlled the basic commodity of land. Married women did not enjoy legal status separate from that of their husbands, nor did minor children apart from their fathers or male guardians. Women's rights to hold property under separate title, to sign contracts, and to divorce and child custody were exceedingly limited, even punitive. Most women of all ranks and origins stepped from the domain of their fathers or male guardians into that of their husbands.

The idea of 'separate spheres' that developed in the early nineteenth century was part of a conservative backlash against the republican notions shaking Europe and America as the revolutionary eighteenth century closed. Separate spheres ideology used the biological differences between women and men to explain other emotional, spiritual, intellectual, and moral differences. Their separate but complementary roles were supposedly designated by God and nature. In fact, this was a value system carefully constructed to reflect the aspirations of an emerging middle class, to reinforce and stabilize its own identity as distinct from the 'decadent' upper classes, and also from the 'great unwashed' below. Home and family represented a strong moral base in the amoral, profit-driven marketplace, an emotional ballast against the strains of the chaotic business world. Through sermons, public addresses, the press, novels, and prescriptive literature, and through the platforms of such organizations as the Woman's Christian Temperance Union, these ideas were widely circulated. The result was a 'cult of domesticity' that tried to confine women to the private sphere, their social and familial roles made synonymous: they were to be dutiful daughters, wives, and mothers.

However forceful their dissemination, ideas do not necessarily indicate how women actually lived. Even the supposedly dependent and idle middle-class woman continued to perform much productive labour in the home, in the absence of the servants necessary to maintain the idealized standards of housekeeping. And working-class and farm women worked as they always had, their family situations still far from the 'male breadwinner' ideal at the heart of the new domesticity. Moreover, women continued to be responsible for charity and church work that brought them out of their sheltered homes and face to face with the dislocations caused by a changing society. In Aboriginal communities, the imposition of such ideas about gender and family greatly upset customary domestic relations. By insisting on male dominance in trapping and trade, formalized monogamous marriage, baptism of children, and patrilineally inherited family names, traders, missionaries, and government officials institutionalized men as 'proper' heads of family and household. The adoption of Western clothing and utensils reinforced the notion of domestic chores as exclusively female responsibilities.

In British North American society on the eve of Confederation, the vast majority of women married, at an average age of twenty-two years. Husbands were commonly a few years older, marrying at an average age of twenty-six years in 1861. They were usually from the community, and of similar religious and socio-economic standing. The choice of spouse and the final decision to wed generally remained with the young couple, but we should not dismiss the influence of religious authority, familial expectations, and community opinion. Courtship was largely a public affair, conducted in family parlours and public places under the watchful eye of kin and neighbours. Betrothal was a formal undertaking, upheld by the law. While these were middle-class practices, strong religious and social proscriptions against premarital sexuality, the severe stigma of illegitimacy, and the notion of 'respectability' among artisans made them more common than not in British North America. Courting men were to ensure that they could support a wife and family independently, and women that they could rely on their suitor's support. The man's ability to provide was also significant in Aboriginal courtship customs. Among the Cree, suitors had to promise the future produce of their hunt to their prospective in-laws until the first child was born and they had proven themselves capable of supporting their families. In Inuit families, suitors first approached parents, who arranged their daughter's marriage if they considered the suitor capable of providing well. Whatever the custom, it was made clear to the young couple that the family and the community had a stake in their union.

Implicit in the glorification of separate spheres was a sexual double standard that ascribed to women a stronger moral rectitude and self-control than men, equipping them to check otherwise 'natural' male sexual compulsions. Paradoxically, women also represented the temptation that both enticed men and brought about their own moral ruin. Only women could fall from grace without hope of salvation. In white colonial society, therefore, marriage was the only socially sanctioned context for sexuality. Sexual relations between married people entailed parenthood as a matter of course. A 'barren' marriage was a cause for much communal head-shaking and finger-wagging. Married women were expected to get pregnant shortly after their weddings, and could look forward to new babies at regular two- or three-year intervals until at least their mid-forties. Families with as many as nine or a dozen children, ranging in age from infancy to young adulthood, were not the 'average' experience, but were certainly not unusual.

In Quebec, both the political power of the Roman Catholic Church and religiosity appear to have increased as the nineteenth century progressed. With growing numbers of priests and female religious communities, the Church was able to develop new social institutions, supported and only minimally regulated by the state. It thereby extended its influence through schools, hospitals, orphanages, poorhouses, homes for the elderly, and all manner of charitable organizations. The deeply conservative ideology of the clergy infused the traditional social elite of the liberal professions, most of them clergy-educated. Their combined efforts on behalf of Catholicism, the French language, and the French-Canadian nation gave much sociocultural weight to the sanctified family and the separate spheres of women and men. As in Protestant English-Canadian circles, organized religion shared with the state a common ideal based on a hierarchical political and social order that made 'the family' its chief cornerstone.

Religious revivals in the early nineteenth century also informed the familial ideology of Protestant English Canada. As family and home became sacred asylums, new ideas about children emanated from press and pulpit that insisted on the parents' duty to shape moral character through careful teaching and example. Although 'mild' forms of corporal punishment remained part of the repertoire of parenting skills, moral regulation through admonition, Bible lessons, repetition, even exhortation, was considered a more effective preventative of bad behaviour. In middle-class homes, where leisure and resources were more abundant, play was also preparation for adult life. The first mass-produced children's toys, appearing around 1860, were miniature wooden versions of adult furniture, horses, carriages, and wagons.

In keeping with 'separate spheres' notions, the domestic roles of ideal mothers and fathers were also distinct but complementary. The husband/father was expected to make all major decisions, whether about finances or about raising the children. Under British Common Law and the Quebec Civil Code, children belonged solely to their father, leaving mothers without legal claim to them in cases of separation, desertion, or divorce. Mothers had no legal recourse, even in widowhood, if fathers chose to will guardianship and custody to another person. The first legal recognition of a mother's claim to her children appeared in Canada West (later Ontario) in 1855, when maternal rights were recognized for children of 'tender years,' or in proven cases of cruelty or desertion. In Quebec, the Civil Code of 1866 also acknowledged the principle of the children's best interests, which meant that the children went to the 'wronged' partner, most often the mother.

Colonial fathers were expected to be affectionate and interested parents, but also to be the disciplinarians and 'governors' of their domain. It was believed that their 'superior' intellectual and rational faculties and public experience made them the proper tutors of their children. Rhetoric aside, women's newly enhanced domestic authority made mothers primarily responsible for the daily work of childrearing. Fathers often took over training and educational plans for adolescents, especially for their sons. By mid-century, paternal authority, as traditionally vested in control of land, household, and craft skills, was becoming increasingly symbolic. As gender images crystallized around 'natural' distinctions between the sexes, mothers came to represent nurturance and selfless devotion, while fathers represented public conceptions of law, order, and authority. Material changes also enlarged the mother's part. With industrial development, more men left their homes to 'work' while women and children stayed behind.

The childrearing customs of Aboriginal peoples were differentiated by region, community organization, spiritual practices, the local economy, and local traditions, among many other factors. For the most part, however, socialization of children was informal and communal, carried out through observation, oral history, and positive example. Tales, games, and more formal ceremonies and rituals taught children about community standards of conduct, inculcated gender roles, and served as rites of passage into adulthood. To teach disobedient children the error of their ways, and to caution them about the likely consequences, discipline was usually administered by shaming or storytelling. Another important distinguishing trait was the Aboriginal respect for autonomy, extended even to young children, that limited to exceptional circumstances the use of force, or the imposition of the adult's will. The corporal punishment, ostracism, and deliberate deprivation common to European childrearing were shocking to the Aboriginal people. A strong cultural disapproval of interference, inquisitiveness, and displays of anger also informed Inuit childrearing practices. Their non-authoritarian approach was linked to their concept of '*ihuma*,' the capacity for rationality and adult maturity that developed as the child grew. Since small children possessed little *ihuma*, they could not be expected to exhibit more rationality and maturity than their years warranted.

By mid-century, idealized domesticity was becoming an important social objective in colonial British North America. This is not to say that the ideal was widely attained. The 'cult of domesticity' was probably limited to the better-off professional and commercial families of colonial society. Any changes effected in its name were also related to the extent of settlement, population density, and socio-economic development in particular regions. A doctor's family in Halifax in 1850, or a lawyer's family in Montreal, would be far more likely to attempt the implied lifestyle than would be the family of a Hamilton artisan or a Prince Edward Island farmer, despite their shared commitment to social respectability. In many homes, the interdependent family economy that characterized preindustrial society was slowly giving way to a similar set of domestic relations in which wage labour and domestic production coexisted. Although the cult of domesticity was meant to be a restful antidote to the emerging industrial order, families could not remain isolated from that order. The new Dominion of Canada would endure convulsive socio-economic change at the turn of the century, slowly emerging from its Victorian colonialism into a self-conscious modernity. The process ignited much public anxiety about wide-ranging 'social problems' which ultimately led all observers back to one: the crisis in the family.

Give-and-Take: Meeting the Changes

This young industrial Canada was a nation in continual

motion. Native-born Canadians and immigrants alike settled
and resettled, in town and city, on northern and western fron-
tiers. Much of this motion involved young people leaving the
countryside in the older central Canadian and Maritime provinces, where good land was becoming scarce, for urban employment or the unsettled expanses of the West. American
settler families also headed northward as their own frontier
closed. The pace increased during the first two decades of
the new century, with the arrival of roughly 3 million prospective Canadians from other nations. Among these were some
half-million immigrants from Asia and southern and central
Europe. Canada's population, at 5.3 million in 1901, increased 43 per cent by 1921. Recent immigrants made up
22 per cent of that total. However much Canada needed immigrants, the newcomers frequently faced a hostility that exacerbated the problems of coping with a new language, culture, and way of life.

Despite its cataclysmic implications, the 'Industrial Revolution' that was making itself felt by the closing quarter of
the nineteenth century is best conceived as an ongoing, un-
even historical process entailing both dramatic change and
significant continuities in life and work, private and public
institutions. Both artisan shops and some degree of domestic production continued alongside the expanding factories.
Some traditional, rural, and preindustrial ways became outmoded, while others were retained, even as they were modified to meet new conditions. If it was not a straightforward
'before and after' affair, there is no doubt that the factory
whistle reordered the relationships within families, and among
families, society, and state. Shopkeeping, artisanal, and farm
families of preindustrial times were labouring units. Many of
these working families continued as such, adapting their traditional strategies and improvising new ones to fit themselves
successfully into the new order. Industrial capitalism also
brought about some reconfiguration of ideas about skill,
gender, and family. Underpinning the 'male breadwinner
family' model that was more and more held up as the 'norm,'

separate-spheres ideology became the most powerful factor restricting women's access to paid labour. Industry's impact on private lives was also matched by its influence on public policy, not only through the political clout of industrial capitalists, but also through social-reform campaigns supporting protective legislation, especially regarding working women and children.

The most discernible change in families was their decreasing size. Ages at marriage began to rise after mid-century, curtailing the total number of childbearing years for women, and therefore the size of families. In 1891 the average age at marriage for women was 23.9 years, and for men 27.2 years. But deliberate family limitation increasingly became a cross-class response to current trends, as land availability declined and the labour of children became less important to family prosperity. Between the first official census of 1851 and the census of 1891, the fertility rate dropped dramatically, from 200 per 1,000 live births to approximately 145. Popular perceptions to the contrary, the decline in fertility was also apparent in Catholic French Canada. French-Canadian mothers in 1861 had an average of about 6.4 children, only slightly higher than the average 6 of English-Canadian mothers; by 1900, the average family size in the province was 4 children. Although Quebec still had Canada's highest birth rate at the turn of the century, much of the province's natural increase was represented by a small number of large rural families.

By the last quarter of the nineteenth century, at least among the more fortunate, enough women were questioning their confinement to hearth and home that the crisis in the family came to be seen as virtually synonymous with the prevailing 'woman question.' Eager to take advantage of the possibilities of the new industrial order, women demanded access to higher education and professional training, and the rights to work, to political representation, and to control their own income and property. Some legislative progress was made in the 1880s, as various provinces expanded property and contractual rights for married women. Political rights had to await the catalyst of global war. If the new day had not yet dawned for women, the turn of the century saw much necessary organization and politicization, and much public debate as to what exactly women's role should be in this developing industrial society.

Ideas and policies governing Aboriginal women also supported the view that their place was with, and determined by, their husbands, imposing a patriarchal, European concept of family on societies to whom it was foreign, and ultimately destructive. In 1876 the Indian Act defined the Aboriginal status of women with exclusive reference to the origins of their fathers and husbands, establishing patrilineage regardless of their tribal traditions. This provision was intended to reduce the number of 'status Indians,' and consequently government responsibility for them. At the same time, it elevated the power and authority of men. The many traditional lineage systems that followed the female line (matrilineage) were simply rejected, Aboriginal women were penalized for marrying outside their culture, and the children of such unions were also denied Indian status. Men could continue to marry as they chose, and their wives and children automatically acquired their status and membership.

New Domestic Realities: Family Life

'Canada's Century' opened to enthusiastic proclamations about a new age signified by advances in science, technology, and industry. There were few visible signs of such 'progress' in the lives of working-class and farm families. A typical male industrial labourer worked about fifty-nine hours a week in 1900. A typical farm woman still laboured ten hours a day in winter and thirteen in summer. A 1913 federal investigative commission on the rising cost of living found that average wages in manufacturing increased 40 per cent between 1900 and 1910 – but the cost of living had risen 50 per cent in the same period, while the wages of the unskilled and of immigrants remained far below the average. Housing costs, which usually consumed the largest proportion of a family's income, had also climbed 60 to 70 per cent in a single decade. Not surprisingly, many of the working poor were badly housed. Griffintown and Saint-Henri in Montreal, Toronto's 'Ward,' the North End in Winnipeg, the East End in Vancouver, Africville in Halifax, and many lesser-known and uncelebrated 'shanty towns' and working-class ghettos were much the same in terms of their rundown, unsanitary environments.

Poverty and racism relegated Native and African-Canadian families, and the families of recently arrived immigrants, to the worst housing of all. Government surveys found Aboriginal families in northern Manitoba living in poorly ventilated and crowded huts. In the 'Cokeville' section of Sydney, Nova Scotia, where the Dominion Steel Company housed the African-American sojourners working its blast furnaces, tax collectors declared the 'coloured quarters' to be 'bad beyond description.' Similar company shacks, without water connections or sewage, were occupied by Hungarians, Poles, and Newfoundlanders. Light and ventilation were frequently inadequate, and existing windows were often sealed or covered to lower fuel costs. In the central district of Toronto that comprised its immigrant, working-class community known as 'the Ward,' only 609 of 2,051 families had bathtubs. Tubs and indoor toilets, however, were rare even in the homes of better-off 'Canadian' workers.

In this material setting, life could be tenuous. Infant, child, and maternal mortality, orphanhood, and early widowhood disrupted between 35 and 40 per cent of all Canadian families. By the time women reached their fifties nearly one-quarter were widowed, compared with about one in ten men; approximately one in six families in 1900 were headed by women alone. In one of Ottawa's working-class wards, fully one-third of every 1,000 infants died before their first birthday. Tuberculosis, the so-called working-man's disease because of its disproportionate incidence in ill-nourished, badly housed, and overworked families, killed more Canadian men and women between the ages of fifteen and forty-five than any other affliction. The tuberculosis death rate among Aboriginals on western reserves was ten to twenty times higher than among non-Aboriginals. For women of childbearing age, maternal mortality was the second-ranked threat to life. Deficiency diseases, such as bone-destroying rickets, were endemic among working-class children, with an estimated incidence as high as 40 per cent.

By 1900, changes in industrial production, the enactment of protective legislation restricting ages and hours of work, and new ideas about childhood came to modify the productive role of children. As their direct economic contribution slowly lessened, earlier trends towards a distinct and protected childhood were formalized. Parents of all ranks increasingly came to value schooling. Late- nineteenth-century reformers redefined childhood as a special stage of institutionalized dependence centred in school attendance and supervised play. More than simply 'malleable,' the child was now depicted as a 'seedling' requiring careful tending, emotional nurture, and protection. Firm parental control and regulation remained important, however, because children could be dangerous as well as endangered. This would be a measured, community-defined control that parents would share with other public institutions, especially the new standardized and age-defined schools.

Old age was also becoming a distinct category in an increasingly categorical social order. Persons aged sixty and over represented just under 8 per cent of Canada's people in 1901. No longer regarded as useful and active participants in an industrial society that lauded efficiency and productivity, the elderly haplessly joined the ranks of other 'social problems.' Demographic shifts and the marginal economic status of working-class families added to the problematic character of old age. With declining fertility and more concentrated childrearing, and as fewer women gave birth in their forties, more children had left home by the time their parents reached old age. Falling birth rates also lowered the ratio of elderly to adult children. It was now more likely for an adult child to have a surviving parent, but fewer siblings to share the burden of care. Elderly women were especially vulnerable to economic distress; slightly over 50 per cent of Canadian women were widowed by ages seventy to seventy-nine.

Many of the elderly, however, still benefited from the pervasive familism that made kin mutually responsible for each other's welfare. In 1900, the majority lived with one of their children. A common family strategy was to share the burden of support among several households within the family, especially if they lived in the same neighbourhood or town. Ageing parents might move in with one child while the others contributed financially, or an elderly person might take turns living with other family members. Among Inuit families in the Yukon, grandparents might winter with one group of children and grandchildren one year, another group the next, so that each domestic unit could maintain a balance between those members who could provide, and those who had to be provided for. In immigrant households, filial deference and family honour dictated that each family take care of its own, whatever the sacrifice entailed. Strong intergenerational attachments in farming and working-class families arose from long-standing patterns of familial inter-dependence. The tendency for adult children to set up their households within proximity of their parents and other family members also sustained these bonds.

The relationship was not necessarily one-sided. The elderly made important contributions to their children's families. Resident grandparents were often responsible for childcare when mothers worked for wages, assisted in farm labour, or were otherwise occupied with heavy domestic duties. They often played influential nurturing roles, filling in for parents whose other pressures left them with little energy for play. A woman growing up in working-class Halifax before the Great War recalled that one of her favourite pastimes was hearing her nana's stories about her own childhood, a cherished bedtime activity for both. The elderly also helped their children financially, and frequently assisted with domestic chores and household repairs and maintenance. Widowed, deserted, and divorced mothers were truly fortunate if they had a parental home to return to with their children, or if parents could move in with them. Respect for the wisdom and experience of elders was integral to Aboriginal cultures, ensuring that family and community accorded them active involvement in childrearing, and the honour and deference regarded as their due. Ultimately, however, the experience of old age depended greatly on the material circumstances of the elderly and their families. The poor, the infirm, and those without supportive kin might well end their years in the House of Refuge, alone and at the mercy of public charity.

The Family That Works Together: Family Economies

In working-class families, and in farm families dependent on occasional wage labour, the shift to industrial modes of production demanded adjustment and innovation in the economic roles of all family members. Wage labour changed the extent to which productive activity characterized family life within the household. Family economies became more dependent on externally earned wages for as many members as possible, particularly fathers and older children. Through group employment in mills and factories, family members continued their preindustrial labour relationship in a transplanted setting, functioning as labour resources, recruitment agents, and a sort of factory police force. Established workers pressured employers to hire family members. In turn, employers counted on older family members to ensure the discipline and productivity of their younger workers. Employers at the Penman's knitting-goods factory in Paris, Ontario, sent home word with family members when they knew of a child, usually a daughter, of working age, and also used kinship networks to encourage emigration of textile workers from England. Despite the rise of scientific management principles, which systematized recruitment, discipline, and labour relations in the name of all-out efficiency, the effectiveness of these traditional kinship connections ensured that they were not completely replaced. Family employment patterns persisted until after the Second World War among women textile workers in Valleyfield, Quebec, as they did among bakery and confectionery workers in Halifax, and among Hamilton steelworkers, to cite only a few examples.

Families with older children who could earn some money fared better than those with young dependants for whom childcare was an additional worry and expense. Some impoverished parents gave up their children, often to relatives, but also to institutions, hoping to retrieve them in better times. Placed in an orphanage with his younger brother until he was fourteen and able to work, a Hamilton man vividly remembered the strict routine, the dull grey uniforms, and the disappointment at not being able to leave when his mother was allowed her weekly visit. All the Protestant orphan homes insisted on both wardship of the children in their care and the right to indenture them at the appropriate age. Many bound the children out when their parents could not pay the fees, often without the parents' knowledge. For these children, labour was not only permissible, it was demanded. The most desperate mothers gave up their children for adoption, often to childless relatives or others looking for help in family businesses and on farms.

Single mothers had few resources beyond their own energies and those of their children, and perhaps supportive kin. Most women were truly 'only a man away from poverty.' A common strategy was to turn the family home into income-producing property by taking in boarders, with children performing cooking and housekeeping chores. A Hamilton woman whose household included eight or nine male boarders at any time remembered the experience poignantly: 'Others were a family. We were a business – it makes a difference ... I always seemed to be so busy working that I never

had time to really make friends.' Another widow did laundry for wealthy people in town, her children carting the baskets back and forth to clients. More fortunate widows were
able to take over their husbands' shops, small businesses, or
trades, or to set up their own enterprises with money received
from the sale of these. A Toronto son of Chinese immigrants
worked alongside his mother and siblings in their small laundry six days a week, often Sundays, until eight or nine o'clock
at night.

If we impose too strict a division between domestic and
productive labour, and define productive labour only as paid
work outside the home, much that went on in families during these years will remain hidden. Typical domestic chores,
such as cooking and laundry, that allow employed members
to replenish themselves and leave for work again the next day
are unpaid but still productive. Other productive domestic
activities, including growing vegetables, baking, raising chickens for meat and eggs, even keeping a cow for milk, were
'paid' in off-the-record ways that tend to evade historians.
Much of the informal 'hidden economy' has historically been
an economy of the marginal, dominated by women and drawing on neighbourhood and kinship networks. Involving reciprocity and payment in kind as well as cash transactions, this
hidden economy is a vital dimension of how ordinary people earned, conserved, and spent irregular and insubstantial
incomes to meet their day-to-day needs. The goods and income brought in by women and children could well make
the difference between family comfort and deprivation. The
competent, capable, respectable working-class housewife had
to be a resourceful manager who 'stretched' family wages with
careful shopping, housekeeping, and creative ways of supplementing income. In Montreal, working-class women frequently planted gardens, baked bread, and raised chickens
and sometimes pigs, both as food and for sale and barter with
neighbours. This pattern of supplementing family income
persisted in smaller towns across Canada through the Second
World War, reviving with the new postwar immigration.

For some marginalized families, the new order brought no real rupture between family, work, and home. 'Separate spheres' did not distinguish public and private so much as they represented the mutuality and reciprocity of all work by family members. From the point of view of those who grew up in the households of the working poor, as one Toronto man remembered, 'the kids just dug in. We could see the earnestness in the way my mother would do it.' Newfoundland fishing families relied heavily on the work of women, whose domestic labour was complicated by the pattern of 'transhumance' based on the seasonal moving of the household. Families living on the exposed headlands often wintered in the head of the bay, taking shelter in crude shacks, or 'tilts,' made habitable by women. Other families lived 'at home' in the winter but moved to 'summer stations' or 'outside' to fish, often hundreds of miles away. Mothers had to pack everything the family might need for four or more months, including food. Feeding the family entailed most of the care of animals and gardens, as well as the ability to 'lay a good table' four times a day. They also worked as 'skippers' in charge of the on-shore fish-drying operation from summer until fall, hiring and supervising labour and managing cash. Wage labour was a defining feature of the lives of African-Canadian women, but they had virtually no legal wage-earning opportunities outside of low-status and ill-paid domestic service, laundry, or sewing, usually in the employ of white middle-class households. Domestic production naturally continued to be important to these families. Rural women in Halifax County gathered wild fruits, berries, and flowers, cultivated an assortment of herbs, roots, and vegetables, and crafted a diversity of small items such as brooms, baskets, and flower boxes, to put up for sale in local markets.

The adoption of machinery for farm production and processing, and the growing commercialization of domestic production, also modified farm family economies. Machinery simplified some operations, changing the gender-definition of certain jobs so that they devolved to women and children, but it also took some skilled jobs away from women. Dairying, a historically important component of farm women's work, was relinquished to farm men and hired labourers as it was commercialized. In other areas, such as the cultivation of fruits and vegetables, women's market participation grew as new urban markets developed and distances were shortened by improved transportation. In general, however, the late-nineteenth-century decline in skilled work for farm women, and the resulting reduction in the money they could earn, left them with little recognized economic input by the developing standards for 'work.' Yet their double-load of farm and domestic labour remained heavy. Rebecca Ells of Kings County, Nova Scotia, managed the family farm with the help of her eighteen-year-old son when her husband joined the Yukon gold rush in 1900. A typical entry for Sunday, traditional day of rest, noted that 'we went down to meeting in the afternoon ... came home, did up the chores, and went again in the Evening ... to Missionary Meeting ... I have just rushed all day.'

Similar trends affected Native families in their traditional fishing, hunting, and gathering economies. Euro-Canadian settlement and the development of railways and highways in British Columbia in the 1910s drew Carrier men into wage labour. Carrier women were often limited to unpaid labour for male kin who held contracts to clear land or produce railway ties. Families nonetheless continued to rely on women's traditional domestic activities in fishing, vegetable farming, tapping, and berry gathering. Ironically, when the federal government banned large salmon weirs in 1911, Carrier fishermen were forced to adopt the net fishing traditionally defined as women's work in their culture. As the catching and preserving of salmon were thus 'feminized,' women's domestic contributions were enlarged because opportunities for men, both in industry and in traditional hunting and trapping, became less reliable. Many also moved into unskilled employment in canning factories, as Native women and children did on the East Coast.

The middle-class model of family life, with its carefully defined gender roles, became increasingly appealing during these years, at least to skilled workers whose commitment to respectability was already well entrenched. Eager to uphold their socio-economic status as the working-class elite, many artisans and their associations publicly espoused such 're-spectable' causes as regular church attendance, temperance, community service, and the male-breadwinner family. Com-posed almost exclusively of skilled tradesmen, labour unions made the 'family wage' a central platform, while urging pro-tective laws that restricted the employment of women and children. In 1884, Ontario was the first province to pass pro-tective legislation prohibiting girls under fourteen and boys under twelve from employment in factory labour, and enforc-ing the ten-hour day and sixty-hour week. Similar legislation was passed by the Quebec Assembly in 1885, and the other provinces thereafter. The result was an even greater distinc-tion between home and work, between the temporary nature of women's wage work and male breadwinning, and between paid productive labour and unpaid reproductive labour. Factory legislation guarded women and children against exploitation, while upholding the belief that women's lives were ideally consecrated to childbearing and childrearing. Whatever the ideals, for many working-class families a single wage was rarely sufficient. The irregularity, seasonality, and gender-typing of employment also ensured the continuity of family interdependence, including child labour. Unable to earn enough to live independently, women continued to need marriage for their material welfare, and could not keep decent full-time jobs once married. They had little choice but to rely heavily on the support of men, and to perform most of the unpaid domestic labour.

Far from preventing women and children from working, in some instances the new labour legislation had the in-advertent effect of making their lives harder. None of the Factory Acts of the 1880s extended their age and hours re-strictions to home work. Mothers and children sometimes

participated in home-centred production as part of a burgeoning 'sweating system,' particularly in textiles and clothing. An 1882 federal government inquiry discovered that 272
of 324 married women workers did most of their work at
home – as much as sixteen hours daily – to avoid the costs of
childcare and to take advantage of the assistance of older
children. A federal investigation in 1896 still found scores of
children working more than sixty hours per week in con-
verted bedrooms, kitchens, and living rooms. Protective legislation addressed the symptoms instead of the causes of child
labour, which were rooted in familial poverty and the nature
of industrial capitalism.

   In factories, in family businesses, on farms, on reserves, or
in the fisheries, working families in industrializing Canada
were organized internally along authoritarian and patriarchal
lines. Living standards and employment outside the home
were directly related to the family's life cycle. There were
moments in its internal history when an appreciable rise in
a family's quality of life was possible, perhaps when a father
and several teenage children held steady jobs, the family was
enjoying good health, and debts were paid down. Also important was the ability of family members to put aside individual desires to work for the larger good of the family. This
mutual dependence opened the way for a measure of coercion, even in cooperative families. Extended schooling and
structural changes were making self-sustaining employment
for older children more difficult to find by the late nineteenth century, so that a growing proportion of children of
all classes were residing with their parents into their late teens
and early twenties. Low wages, lack of alternatives, and family loyalty probably kept the majority of daughters and many
sons with their parents until they were married, affecting the
timing of individual and family life-stages, but also increasing the likelihood of intergenerational conflict. No matter
what the extent of their contribution, wives and children were
dependent upon, and subordinate to, the male head of
household. This familial authority may well have been the
only source of power allowed to working-class men in a sys-

tem that subordinated them on every other level. The industrial workplace replicated these power relations in its own structures, at once reflecting and reinforcing both the traditional domestic hierarchy and the newer notion of distinctly separate spheres for women and men.

Families in Motion: Migration and Immigration

As good land became increasingly scarce in the older settled provinces of central and Eastern Canada, the dream of land ownership eluded many families. Younger members of established farm families were often obliged to seek their fortunes elsewhere. When local employment opportunities failed to meet the needs of farm families for supplementary income, family migration became a viable strategy. The movement of French Canadians to the factories of Maine and New England provides a clear example of this particular strategy. Children were employed in the New England textile mills for an average of seventy-two hours a week throughout the year, while male employment was sporadic and seasonal, a dramatic change from the traditional farm-family economy. Increasing work opportunities in Quebec slowed the outward flow by 1900, but 10,000 Quebeckers still left for New England in that year alone, much to the consternation of the Church and nationalist authorities. The stagnation of trade and industry that affected late-nineteenth-century Nova Scotia meant that many young men in the town of Canning stayed in school until they were between the ages of sixteen and eighteen, and could not establish separate households until they were twenty-six or twenty-seven years old. Given the near-impossibility of their own financial independence, young women continued to marry at the relatively early age of twenty-one or twenty-two. The only other significant option for many young Maritimers, as for young Quebeckers, was out-migration. Between the 1860s and 1890s, at least a quarter of a million people – one in three adults – left the Maritimes in search of employment, including roughly 150,000 women.

Whether accompanied by family or on their own, many of those arriving in Canada during these years were motivated by family needs and ambitions. Some of these immigrants were sojourners, 'target migrants' intending to stay only long enough to improve their families' material situation in their countries of origin. Many were married men and fathers. The regular cash remittances that they posted to their families made them as much 'breadwinners' as though they were physically present in their households. Married or single, the sojourners were weighted with enormous responsibility for meeting their families' material expectations. The process of 'chain migration,' based on networks of family and kin, facilitated the quest for new opportunities. Kinship networks provided crucial assistance with employment, housing, childcare and finances, often making all the difference between permanent settlement and the decision to return to whatever starting place was home. Bad luck, betrayal, and exploitation by dishonest employers, economic downturns, accidents and ill health, could impede or abort a sojourn. The results might be personal indebtedness and deprivation, prolonged separation, family breakdown, and the kind of psychic toll only hinted at in the statistics for suicide, alcoholism, violence, and mental illness. Contact was sometimes lost, accidentally or deliberately. For those deemed 'racially undesirable,' official immigration policy also deliberately thwarted the establishment of new families, or the resettlement of existing ones. After the railway-building boom of the late nineteenth century, Chinese and South Asian immigration was severely restricted through the imposition of a high 'head tax,' and other discriminatory measures. These policies effectively achieved their purpose of blocking the reproduction of Chinese and South Asian families. In the census of 1911, these immigrant communities were almost exclusively male.

Home ownership was a priority for many European immigrants, who regarded the family home as property in common, a stable, concrete, economic foundation for domestic respectability and prosperity. Often the family financed its purchase by taking in boarders, usually single men from its own ethnic group. Running a boarding house permitted women to contribute to the family income without working outside the home, a point of honour in many immigrant families. Conditions were rarely more luxurious in these private boarding houses than in the commercial ones. One Ukrainian immigrant family of seven settled in a three-room shack in Saskatoon in 1911. The entire family shared one room, while six male boarders slept in three beds in another, and one or two others slept in the small kitchen. Reform-minded Canadians were much disturbed by this evidence of ethnic overcrowding, with its threats to the physical and moral health of both 'foreigners' and their own families. The immigrants' immediate concerns were practical ones: shelter, proximity to kin and fellow immigrants, and saving money. Inconveniences were temporary sacrifices on the path to an improved situation, in either this or the old country. Kinship ties could also operate as effective moral safeguards, making individuals accountable for their behaviour, if only because they knew that news would get back to their families and bring dishonour to them. The communities that 'Canadian' observers tended to classify as slums, as visible and disturbing evidence of urban pathology, were resources for mutual aid and solidarity that often gave their residents their only protection against the hostile society surrounding them.

Immigrant families were among the last to be able to afford the segregation of function and private life that was gradually becoming characteristic of North American industrial society. The distinction between public and private, between home and work, was a luxury. Children who lacked private yards and public playgrounds appeared to be always on the streets. Neighbours in crowded quarters visited on front stoops or porches. Men met other men for camaraderie in old-country cafés, barber shops, and taverns. Lacking facilities to store large quantities of food and other necessities, immigrant women shopped daily, often using the rare opportunity to shake loose their domestic confines and catch up on news with shopkeepers and other shoppers. This street activity, transplanted and modified from its original village setting, was simply too public for middle-class Canadians who sanctified domestic privacy. It represented only noise, dirt, congestion, and the potential for trouble symbolized by 'uncivilized' and 'inferior' people from other lands.

Similarly, differentiation of family roles, and any sense of individual rights taking priority over family goals, were neither economically possible nor culturally acceptable in many immigrant families. The immigrant parents' attitude towards child labour was rooted in material need, but also in traditional ethnic and religious understandings of family. Protected and protracted childhood was frivolous in their circumstances. The central domestic role of the wife/mother, patriarchal authority, family loyalty and filial obedience, all denoted an abiding sense of 'family honour.' Immigrant families functioned as corporate groups, but familial cooperation did not mean egalitarianism. Female members of all ages were subordinate to the male head of household and older sons, although reverence for mothers and protectiveness towards sisters could mitigate the worst possibilities of that subordination. These family roles and relations were sustained by the rules and rituals of transplanted Roman Catholic, Greek Orthodox, and Jewish faiths.

Most immigrant parents recognized the value of learning English as quickly as possible. Most immigrant children, especially the younger ones who attended school, would always have greater facility with the language than would their parents. This could lead to distancing between parent and child, who literally spoke in different tongues, and also to a curious role-reversal in which the child effectively parented its own parents by mediating many day-to-day transactions, from dealing with doctors and visiting social workers to paying bills. The children of immigrants were regarded as more Canadian than their parents. Yet, to be Canadian, they had to be different from their parents. There was an uneasy ambivalence underlying parent–child relations in many immigrant families. This tension between the Old World, represented by parents, and the New World which demanded their adaptation in ways that often required 'Anglo-conformity,' was as much a part of the immigrant family experience as were the more immediate adjustments necessitated by the new material setting of their lives. A Macedonian girl growing up in Toronto remembered that, 'when I was a kid we were so scared of my dad that we would wait two weeks before we had enough nerve to ask him if we could go to a movie. We could never do anything ... always had to be with our parents.' But she held no grudge against him because she believed that he 'just didn't seem to know that in Canada you don't have to act that way with your kids.'

Parents may have accepted that becoming Canadian was crucial to their children's success, and therefore familial success, but still resented the challenge to family relations and ethnic customs that these changes posed. If Canadians were inclined to regard immigrant parents as callous, harsh, and exploitative, immigrants saw an individualism in Canadian families that bespoke lack of respect for parents and older family members, and a coldness that revealed the absence of affective ties between parents and children, between siblings, and among kin.

Cradle of the Nation: Prairie Families

Home to diverse Aboriginal and Métis families, the great Northwest was considered 'unsettled' as long as it was not settled by white families. Although many newcomers ended up swelling the ranks of the urban proletariat, the true intent of John A. Macdonald's National Policy of 1879 was to populate the West as an agrarian hinterland to the central Canadian manufacturing core. Taking up the cause with fervour, the Liberal government of Wilfrid Laurier actively encouraged immigration. To understand the centrality of family on the homesteading frontier, we need only recall the famous words of Laurier's Minister of the Interior, Clifford Sifton, invoking the arrival of the 'stalwart peasant in a sheepskin coat.' The less-cited remainder of this familiar quote refers to the 'good quality,' in the day's racist terms, represented by the ideal immigrant and his 'stout wife and half a dozen children.' The Prairie provinces were the metaphoric cradle of the nation, the specific site of intentional, planned, and carefully promoted nation-building.

Marriage and family were thus the key institutions of prairie agriculture, fostering material success, social stability, and conservative values. Only women with dependent children were permitted to homestead on their own; the unattached non-mother was not an acceptable or welcome farmer. 'Bachelorhood' was considered a temporary and clearly problematic way of life. With the costs of labour and provisions subsumed in their production, the economic contribution of farm-family members was immeasurable. On the whole, families were larger than in urban settings, even for homesteaders of 'Canadian' or British origins. Among such sectarian groups as the Mennonites, Doukhobors, and Hutterites, the family was the basis of the solid communities that they transferred virtually intact from their Old World setting, the principal instrument of adaptation.

The agrarian frontier potentially offered a more equitable partnership between pioneering women and men, in that necessity obliged couples to share the burdens of settlement. Whatever the initial promise, conventional gender ascriptions, with their corresponding divisions of labour and inequality of status, won out. Mechanization of threshing and harvesting helped to ease some of the heavy toil of men, but most of the work allotted to women did not benefit from the advantages of technology. The prairie farm wife spent long days performing the usual household chores: hauling firewood and water to the house, scrubbing laundry against zinc washboards, and making soap and candles from bacon, lard, and bone marrow. Women and children passed many additional hours in the 'farm work' of cleaning barns and chicken coops, caring for poultry, collecting eggs and churning butter for household use and sale, and gardening. The pressures of homesteading obliged them to attempt such tasks as house-building. Twelve years old when his family settled in Battleford, Saskatchewan, in 1907, one English immigrant recalled the herculean labour demanded for survival: 'I worked on that house because we needed that roof over our heads before winter. Mother had never done anything more strenuous than drive a pony cart or do embroidery or pick flowers and here she was, up on the roof with rope tied around her skirt on each side so the legs wouldn't show just in case a neighbour came along.' The centrality of family labour was taken for granted. As another man noted, 'it wasn't exactly that we called it work, it was more like just part of our lives. By about nine I was doing a man's job with the cows ... when you would be twelve you'd pretty well given up the business of school.'

The subjugation of Aboriginal communities was also fundamental to the federal government's aim of re-creating 'Canada' in the West through immigration and the free homestead system. To that end, seven land treaties were negotiated between 1871 and 1877. The railway and the North West Mounted Police were firmly ensconced by 1883. With the Native/Métis resistance that flared in the Riel Rebellion of 1885 ruthlessly crushed, all that remained was for the Natives to be placed on their federally decreed 'reserves' and turned into productive farmers and efficient housewives. Government policy deliberately promoted subsistence farming. Various regulations, most notably certain 'pass laws,' prevented Natives from leaving the reserves to sell goods at market. Such regulations were particularly aimed at restraining Native women, interfering with their ability to provide adequately for their families. When they failed to measure up to government expectations, largely because the training and provision were inadequate to the task, they were castigated for their supposedly innate, racially determined inability to 'settle.' Officials believed that Native men were incapable of providing for their families except in the outmoded manner of hunters, warriors, and nomads, and that women were dissolute, immoral, and somehow responsible for the deplorable housing on reserves, the high mortality rate, the neglected and 'rebellious' children, and the general poverty. But these families were allotted one-room huts that had poor ventilation, dirt floors, and walls of mud and hay, homes that were unhealthy and impossible to keep clean. Shortages of food and basic clothing were common.

The prejudiced views of government agents obscure what other sources tell us: namely, that, in the early reserve years and especially after the Rebellion, women provided essential security and stability in Aboriginal communities suffering from defeat and hopelessness. They were also helpful to new settlers, teaching them how to use edible plants and other native materials for nourishment and medicine, and assisting women at childbirth. But the arrival of white women effectively ended the long-standing practice of intermarriage according to the 'custom of the country,' as white men began to leave their Aboriginal families for new unions with white women. Previously upheld in Canadian courts, the validity of these mixed marriages was negated in 1886, when it was decided that the 'cohabitation of a civilized man and a savage woman,' for no matter how long, was not legal marriage. Children were thereby disentitled from their father's estate. The children of the first marriage most often lived in poverty with their mothers on the reserve. Even when they were provided for by white fathers, they were not accepted into white communities. Racial prejudice, inscribed in the various Indian Acts, 'decultured' and undermined these Aboriginal families, who were judged against an inflexible white, middle-class, Euro-Canadian ideal.

Conclusion

Socio-economic pressures demanded resourceful adaptations on the part of families in the industrial Canada that was developing between 1850 and 1914. Despite the dislocations that modernizing forces brought in their wake, and widespread fears that family bonds would dissolve, familial adjustments were often based on earlier customs of mutual assistance and interdependence that relied strongly on just those bonds. These were the relations that remained reliable within an otherwise unstable environment. Thus, if some older patterns of family living were discarded, many were retained, if modified to meet new circumstances.

The structural changes marking this period were accelerated by the exigencies of the world war that began in 1914. Accompanying social stresses made the problems afflicting families appear more ominous 'than ever before,' a point of comparison that would haunt public debates well into the interwar years. The give-and-take process of family change slowly deprived married women of their central role in domestic production, and identified fathering with providing, childhood with schooling, and adolescence with prolonged familial dependence. Comprising a breadwinner father, a stay-at-home mother, and dependent children in school, the middle-class family model became a benchmark of personal respectability and national success. In a period devoted to nation-building, measuring up to its demands was the 'respectable' family's responsibility to society.

2

Mending Crisis-Torn Families:
Reform and Regulation

As we have seen, by the last quarter of the nineteenth century, changes in production and social organization were demanding certain adjustments on the part of Canadian families, and also fuelling public anxieties. Worried observers feared that industrialization, urbanization, and immigration, if left unregulated, might disrupt their comfortable neighbourhoods, and that they would be powerless to protect their 'Canadian' families from what they invariably saw as negative influences. Fears about social degeneration were inflamed by the mass arrival of immigrant families, their high birth rate relative to the decreasing size of 'Canadian' families, and continuing high infant mortality. Since women's roles and identities were rooted in family, the movement of women into paid labour was also shaking society at its core. Perhaps more frightening than the real, material difficulties faced by many Canadian families of this time, therefore, was this sense of foreboding about the collapse of cherished social institutions and relations, including 'the family' itself.

This chapter focuses on reformist attempts to address the family crisis that appeared to be a direct result of the massive structural changes taking place during this transformative period. These were years of burgeoning public involvement in social and moral reform, much of it organized under the auspices of the Social Gospel. Espousing an activist Christianity, the Social Gospel was largely a middle-class, urban,

Protestant movement that attended to the worst abuses of industrial capitalism in the interest of achieving a just and orderly 'New Jerusalem.' In Quebec, Pope Leo XIII's encyclical *Rerum Novarum* (1891), condemning uncontrolled capitalism, sparked similar activities among Catholics.

To protect their society and the families at its base, reformers asserted rules for proper family relations, and encouraged public surveillance of families to see that these were followed. The crisis that they identified hinged on the great divide between their own middle-class family lives and those of other Canadians. Yet it was just as much about the gap between the ideal family – the family as it ought to be – and families as they actually existed. Convinced that social problems were increasing at an alarming rate, reformers blamed pathological families, directly linking 'broken homes,' sexual immorality, juvenile delinquency, and violence. Racist ideas derived from the pseudo science of eugenics, which constructed an elaborate racial hierarchy that placed white Anglo-Celtics at the very top, also influenced prevailing family-crisis theories. By the outbreak of the Great War, the ideal family – in the minds of social reformers, many of them professionals employed in expanding education, health, and welfare fields – was clearly a projection of their own middle-class experiences and ambitions.

**Maternal Feminism and Family-Centred Reform:
Saving Children**

By the 1870s, a variety of middle-class women's organizations were concerned about the problems of family life among the working poor. Volunteer women were instrumental in the establishment of such institutions as the Protestant Children's Homes in Montreal, Kingston, Toronto, and Halifax. The Woman's Christian Temperance Union, founded in Ontario in 1874, expanded the pre-Confederation campaign against alcohol and its ravages on family life. The creation of the National Council of Women of Canada in 1893 signalled the

hope, enthusiasm, and experience that women brought to
the cause of child and family welfare. Building on the foundations of their traditional philanthropic activities, middle-
class women reformers used the domestic imagery of light,
soap, and water to portray themselves as the nation's housekeepers, intent on 'sweeping' out the cobwebs of corruption;
'shining light' on dark corners of poverty, evil, and immorality; and 'cleansing' society of its 'infections.' Through
public campaigns, some were able to make a place for themselves in 'feminine' professions such as teaching, nursing, and
social work. Also formally initiated in the 1870s, the suffrage
cause gained much from their new social activism, indicating that women could use separate spheres ideology to their
own advantage.

In addition to the groups organized specifically by and for
women, other national reform organizations included a large
contingent of women in their membership. The most influential of these was the Moral and Social Reform Council of
Canada (1907), effectively the first national social-work organization, which became the Social Service Council in 1913.
The self-defined mandate of such groups was to guide families through the turmoil of adjustment to socio-economic
change and, intact and strengthened, out the other side. The
period's focus on nation-building connected specific definitions of domestic virtue with national stability, supplying
further reason for public involvement in family lives. For
women, however, the maternalist premise of most reform
campaigns was ultimately limiting, leaving little room for any
real expansion of their sphere beyond the family and family-
related social concerns.

Much as was the case internationally, many of these reform
groups campaigned in support of child welfare as a key component of the health, broadly defined, of family and nation.
Their immediate purpose was to reduce the horrific infant
mortality rates that saw one in five Canadian babies in 1900
dying before the end of its first year. Available statistics confirmed that this was a class mortality. The families of indus-

trial workers appeared to be the first casualties of the new order. A series of infant mortality reports, produced for the Ontario government by Dr Helen MacMurchy between 1911 and 1913, revealed that the foremost killers of infants were such preventable scourges as diarrhoea and enteritis (*cholera infantum*). Although their exact cause was not yet established, it was known that contaminated milk was the prime source. Thus MacMurchy led child-welfare advocates in insisting that maternal breastfeeding was the best solution. They also insisted that the problem of infant mortality could be resolved only through state involvement.

Organized by local women's groups under the supervision of medical volunteers, pure-milk depots were established in urban areas in English Canada by the early 1900s. Like the *Gouttes de lait* in Quebec, also initiated in these years, they were intended to distribute pure milk to families that could not otherwise afford it, at a time when pasteurization was rare and its value still disputed. As the medical profession came to espouse maternal education and supervision as crucial to the infant-mortality crusade, these depots evolved into all-round 'well baby' clinics. The clinics were supervisory and diagnostic, and were never meant to provide medical treatment. Though clinics were usually staffed by nurses, attendant doctors advised mothers on daily care and routines, weighed babies, noted progress or any problems, and urged regular visits to private physicians – despite the fact that most of these mothers were unable to afford any but emergency medical care for their families. Doctors increasingly explained high infant mortality rates as a failure of motherhood. Their 'scientific' constructions of normal womanhood reinforced the 'family values' derived from their own class backgrounds. In Quebec, doctors were important members of the conservative clerico-nationalist elite, actively supporting the Church in its glorification of familism and maternity. Across the nation, doctors contended that the poor, particularly those classified 'inferior' by virtue of ethnicity and race, were refusing to take responsibility for their own health and that of their children. That infant mortality in Aboriginal communities was almost twice as high as in other Canadian communities, and three times as high among the Inuit, was interpreted as evidence of ignorance and racial inferiority, rather than poverty and lack of medical care.

By 1914, many municipal governments had taken over the operation of clinics as part of their expanding public-health work. Visiting nurses were sent out by municipal health departments to deliver the message to new mothers in their homes, to check on the domestic environment, and to give 'demonstrations' on good housekeeping and the proper care of children. In addition to the government-employed nurses, private organizations such as the Victorian Order of Nurses and the Red Cross Society took active part in home visiting, especially in rural and sparsely settled outpost districts. In Quebec, where the state was slower to get involved, the Metropolitan Insurance Company began sending nurses to the homes of working-class clients in 1909. The nurses helped mothers prepare for home births in the most hygienic conditions possible, and advised on infant care. On the whole, mothers appreciated these efforts for their families, despite their intrusive aspects. Especially in isolated districts, mothers far from family and friends looked to visiting nurses as 'angels of mercy.' The nurses' field reports noted that most mothers approached were eager to learn the best ways of caring for their families. Indeed, given the high price of ill health among those who could not afford medical care, prevention was often truly the only viable approach.

Remaking Deviant Families: Scientific Childrearing

The rising swell of reform activity, and corresponding calls for government intervention, prompted official state inquiries into various areas of public concern. These inquiries, dealing not only with health issues, but also with labour, crime, and education, questioned the traditional assumption that parents knew their children's best interests and that the state had little business interfering in private homes. Until the late nineteenth century, the state's explicit role as protector of children was limited to the prohibition of infanticide and severe physical abuse. The developing view was that 'society' should decide the standards for effective parenting and a proper home life. A series of new laws specified certain minimal legal, economic, and moral criteria to ensure the necessary conditions for child welfare, and to establish guidelines for the health, education, and behaviour of children. The nation-building process suggested the possibility of defining an ideal citizen. The key to making that exemplary Canadian lay with the care and protection of 'normal' children, not just those regarded as 'deviant' and needy, through legislation and other state initiatives to influence domestic lives and private relations.

Beginning with Ontario in 1871, by 1905 all provinces except Quebec had laws requiring children between the ages of seven and fourteen years to go to school for certain minimum periods. Although most working-class and farm children continued to finish before their fourteenth birthdays, school was gradually replacing apprenticeship, domestic service, and other full-time wage labour for young adolescents. Canadian children were typically spending almost eight years in school by 1911. Only slightly more than 44 per cent of all fifteen-year-olds, however, actually attended school in that year. Attendance continued to be shaped by the family's economic needs and the nature of the local labour market. The common experience was a moving in and out of the classroom, as parents kept children home to mind younger siblings, take on temporary employment, or help out in various ways. Youngsters from the middle and upper classes still enjoyed their traditional advantage. 'If you went to school after you were fourteen,' recalled a man growing up in Hamilton in the early twentieth century, 'your old man was either a banker or a brewer or he owned a store or was quite wealthy.'

Formal schooling became more important than ever in shaping model children. The school, it was theorized, would fill whatever void was created by the perceived flaws in family life. Reformers hailed education as the key to resolving all social problems and the cornerstone of the cooperative, Christian commonwealth to which they aspired. Like family, school and work were intended to be critical agents of socialization and social reproduction. The introduction of 'manual training' for boys and 'domestic science' for girls by 1900 reinforced the notion of school as preparation for adult life, and affirmed that public and private roles were biologically determined. Children of 'foreign' and Aboriginal families would learn to speak English, be Christian (preferably Protestant), adopt middle-class standards of hygiene and family values, and acquire attitudes conducive to productivity and citizenship. Schools purposely taught children to accept and embrace social identities defined by class, gender, and 'race.'

When the land treaties of the 1870s effectively made Native peoples wards of the state, the educational system became the key to 'reforming' them for the purposes of their white 'superiors.' While the treaties promised schools 'on reserve,' residential schools – many at a considerable distance – were believed to be the most effective countervailing force to 'deficient' Aboriginal homes. Indian Act amendments in 1895 made attendance compulsory, authorizing justices or Indian agents to commit Aboriginal children under the age of sixteen years to industrial schools or boarding schools. Conditions at the schools were frequently poor, seriously undermining the children's health. Deaths from childhood diseases and tuberculosis were so common that Duncan Campbell Scott, Deputy Minister of Indian Affairs, estimated that 50 per cent of the children who entered the schools did not live to benefit from their education. In addition to the emotional scars inflicted by the forced separation of young children and parents, and the cultural breakdown wrought by the goals of assimilation and conversion, physical, emotional, and sexual abuse were tragically common. Those who survived entered a society that would not acknowledge their experiences, condemning Aboriginal families to relive the nightmare across succeeding generations.

The shift in focus from parental rights to parental responsibilities and children's rights was facilitated by legislative departures and the creation of institutions to enforce new child-welfare policies. Acting on behalf of neglected, abused, and abandoned children, the Ontario Children's Aid Society (CAS; 1891), which developed out of the Toronto Humane Society, eventually became a nationwide network. The Ontario government sanctioned the activities of the CAS with the passage of the Children's Protection Act in 1893. Due in large part to the unflinching efforts of John Joseph Kelso, journalist, social activist, and first Ontario Superintendent of Neglected and Dependent Children, most provinces had joined the CAS network with enabling legislation and their own provincial agencies by 1901. By 1913, Ontario welfare statutes detailed twelve different conditions for state custody of children, including the immoral conduct of parents or 'permitting or encouraging a child to violate curfew, begging, vagrancy and labour laws.' The solution to a bad home environment was removal of the child, and frequently prosecution of the parents. The majority of the 600 children placed in foster homes annually between 1910 and 1913 were neither orphaned nor abandoned, but apprehended by the CAS from 'undesirable homes.' By the outbreak of the First World War, the CAS had transformed itself from a voluntarist and philanthropic coalition of 'child-savers' to a powerful regulatory agency, staffed largely by professional social workers who kept an eye on 'bad' homes and enforced legislation.

The subject of 'problem youth' added another angle to public anxiety about 'the family besieged.' Crowding city streets in barely respectable occupations, hawking wares, selling newspapers, delivering messages and goods, lounging about billiard halls and penny theatres, working-class boys appeared a growing social menace. In 1885, a Toronto police survey enumerated about 700 youngsters, mostly boys, who regularly participated in the street trades; 175 newsboys and a few girls were working the streets of Ottawa in 1890. Concerned citizens established 'newsboys' homes' in such cities, where these 'strays' could be sheltered and supervised, as much to keep them out of criminal activity as to protect their health and welfare. By the early twentieth century, when jobs in retail, services, and offices expanded across the country, the increasing numbers of young unmarried women heading out on their own for the cities provoked fears about a corresponding 'girl problem.' In 1912 a Montreal social worker claimed to have personally counted, on a single week night, 125 girls under age sixteen 'out unattended, promenading up and down' at the corner of St-Laurent and Ste-Catherine streets. Overall, public discussions suggest an ambivalence about whether boys or girls posed the greater threat, needed the greater attention and intervention, or promised the greater remedial capacity. It was clear to reformers that there was 'a problem concerning adolescents primarily,' and that the need for intervention was 'proportionately greater' in working-class and immigrant quarters.

With their sights fixed on these young people, educators, doctors, and those newly trained in 'social service,' many of them involved in Social Gospel, embraced the theories of American psychologist G. Stanley Hall. Hall's authoritative text, *Adolescence: Its Psychology and Its Relation to Physiology, Anthropology, Sociology, Sex, Crime, Religion, and Education* (1904), portrayed biological puberty as a time of moral, sexual, and psychological upheaval. During this turbulent life-stage, young people were vulnerable to the corruptions and temptations of the adult world, and ill-equipped to deal with them. Material changes had also unleashed new demons. With growing factory production and the decline of a masculine, work-based culture, young workers of both sexes gained access to more jobs, more and freer contact at work and outside, some money of their own, and the ability to buy 'fun.' Urbanization and new technologies provided com-

mercialized – and unsupervised – opportunities for amuse-
ment. If this meant little real change in the economic status
of adolescents, in that most were still unable to leave the parental home, it marked significant change in familial relations. Parents were increasingly unable to 'provide' for
their children's futures through the transmission of family
property, trades, or businesses. Their influence on adolescent
attitudes and behaviours lessened, even as their direct economic responsibility for their children was extended to early
adulthood.

The Laurier government's Royal Commission on Industrial
Education and Vocational Training (1908–11) strove to define adequate substitutes for apprenticeship and other traditional methods of training and regulating the young. At the
same time, a tremendous upsurge in organizational activity
for young people, including the Boy Scouts and Girl Guides,
the newly devised Tuxis and Trail Rangers for boys, and the
Canadian Girls in Training, also attempted to provide 'healthy'
outlets for the youthful 'gang instinct.' Worries about 'the
youth problem' inspired such measures as the federal Juvenile Delinquents Act of 1908. By establishing a whole new
category of youthful lawbreakers, the act added another
potentially coercive edge to state regulation of family life
among the working and dependent poor. The state enlarged
its parental role at the same time that it tried to reinforce
families through the creation of special socialized children's
courts. For the first time in history, a child could be legally
censured for non-criminal behaviours such as truancy, wan-
dering, and loitering, and also for engaging in 'adult' practices, particularly gambling, drinking, smoking, and sex.
Together with the various provincial children's protection
acts, this legislation greatly increased the numbers of children
and parents who could be charged for failure to measure up
to the new standards of family life. Most of the families regarded as 'inadequate' were of immigrant, Aboriginal, and
working-class origins, assuring child-savers of the righteous-
ness of their mission.

The White Life for All: Moral Regulation

There were many other attempts to remake 'deviant' families in the interests of nation-building. The Protestant churches initiated evangelical, educational, and medical missions in immigrant neighbourhoods across Canada. The Methodist Women's Missionary Society, which opened its first mission to Alberta's Ukrainian immigrants in 1904, used Sunday schools to improve the children's English and transmit 'Canadian' morals, religious principles, and family values through them to their homes. In the summer of 1910, the University of Toronto set up the first of three 'settlement houses,' modelled on London's famous Toynbee Hall and Chicago's Hull House. Established in the city's most congested poor neighbourhoods – described in promotional literature as consisting of 'large families of labouring people'– the settlements allowed social-work students to combine study of urban slums with social service. Their primary purpose was to train immigrants in the duties of citizenship, with special efforts extended to the children, who were identified as 'Canadians in the making.'

Attempts to regulate private relations and reproduction held much appeal in influential social and political circles, testifying to the depth of middle-class anxiety about the 'crisis in the family' that was unravelling the social fabric. Building on its earlier temperance foundations, especially through the efforts of the Woman's Christian Temperance Union (WCTU), the early twentieth-century prohibition movement also focused on depraved 'foreign' and working-class homes, encouraging facile correlations about immigrant alcohol use, sexual licence, immorality, and inferiority. Reformist interest in eugenics, a pseudo science inspired by Darwinism and premised on the notion of 'selective breeding,' led to anti-contraception campaigns, since family limitation was perceived to be largely a practice of the 'better stock.' Eugenicists also supported crusades to restrict marriage by raising the legal age, requiring medical certificates, and tightening licensing; avidly pro-natalist infant-welfare drives; and proposals for the segregation and sterilization of the 'unfit.' 'Unfitness' became a medical/moral category applied judgmentally to a frightening array of those considered 'unfit' by those who considered themselves fit to judge.

Views such as these often intersected with campaigns promoting 'social purity,' or 'the white life for two,' generally through attacks on male promiscuity and attempts to confine sexual relations to lawfully married heterosexual couples. Social-purity activists invoked the state's duty to enter the bedrooms of the nation in the interests of a regenerated society based on traditional family and gender relations, and especially feminine morality. The Society for the Protection of Women and Children used such arguments to influence the 1892 amendments to the Criminal Code, which elaborated a comprehensive system of offences to protect the sexual innocence of women and enforce a stringent code of sexual behaviour. Abortion, contraception, and 'seduction' were criminalized. All sexual acts between men were classified as 'gross indecency.' While attacks on the double standard and legislative protection from sexual violence and exploitation were clearly beneficial to women, they were based on ideas about their ordained moral superiority and maternal vocation. The overall result, therefore, was conservative and repressive.

Social-purity advice literature circulated widely, and lectures and classroom talks were heard by thousands. The best-selling sex-information literature in Canada between 1900 and 1915 was contained in the eight volumes of the 'Self and Sex' series, produced and distributed by doctors and Protestant clergy. These advice manuals featured the 'limited energy' theory, which stressed the importance of restricting sexuality for the sake of personal health and healthy reproduction, hence 'racial' or national health. Ominous euphemisms such as 'solitary vice' and 'self-abuse' equated masturbation with waste and corruption, at once sources and symptoms of moral and physical decay that would probably lead to dissipation, insanity, and early death, or – even worse – to the perpetuation of physical and mental weakness across generations. Medical professionals and social critics also paid closer, if still circuitous, attention to the 'evil' of 'unnatural' same-sex relationships. The medical author of *What a Young Girl Ought to Know* warned about the 'fondling and gushing' between girls that might lead to a 'weakening of moral fibre' and the degeneration of friendship into 'a species of self-abuse.'

Family-focused reform campaigns also directed public attention to wife-battering and child abuse, which were presented as if they were exclusively problems of working-class and immigrant families. Available contemporary reports, mostly from court records, indicate that violence was an all-too-common aspect of family life that did not respect class or ethnic boundaries. Religious and legal structures supported the subordination of wives and children, who were thus subject to the will of husbands and fathers. As the most subordinate of all human beings, children owed their protection almost exclusively to the very parents or guardians who could also be the primary threats to their health and well-being. A 'reasonable' amount of physical punishment was not considered inappropriate.

Adding human beings to its agenda in the 1880s, the Society for the Prevention of Cruelty to Animals (SPCA) publicized the evils of domestic violence, and provided practical, legal, and moral support to battered women. Although women did attempt to protect themselves and to get legal redress, they suffered much pain and terror before going to the authorities, and were more often motivated by the man's failure to provide than by his violent behaviour. Even in cases of brutal assault and obvious guilt, the courts continued to mete out ludicrously short sentences, and provided no aid to the victims. Law and society averted their eyes to protect the public image of the patriarchal family. In any event, incarcerating the family's principal earner might have spared women and children from violence, but the tremendous odds against survival faced by woman-headed families must have made this solution a mixed blessing.

Despite what reformers took to be mounting evidence of family crisis, and despite their willingness to advocate state involvement to 'fix' the family's problems, they drew the line at divorce reform. The inflexible divorce law was another available means to enforce particular standards of morality, domestic life, and sexual conduct, strengthening 'norms' and actively establishing the hegemony of the middle-class family model. In Quebec, the Civil Code forbade divorce, although after Confederation it was possible to override the prohibition by a federal statute granting parliamentary divorce, as in English Canada. The Church, however, refused to recognize parliamentary divorce, invoking excommunication for Catholics who attempted remarriage. The threatened penalties and intrinsic difficulties evidently worked. The number of divorce applications in Quebec actually declined in each decade of this period. In all Canada, there were only 213 divorces, an average of just over 9 per year, between 1870 and 1900.

Given the expense and trouble, many more couples than statistics can show simply agreed to part, and made their own arrangements for child custody and support. Some reconstituted their families through new common-law partnerships, usually kept from public knowledge. And simple desertion came to be known as 'the poor man's [and, to a lesser extent, woman's] divorce.'

Conclusion

By the outbreak of war in 1914, the men, women, and children of the young Dominion represented a multitude of religious, cultural, and national backgrounds. These differences, complicated by specific material circumstances, shaped attitudes towards marriage, family, childrearing, and the labour of women and children that were sometimes distinct from those idealized by middle-class 'Canadians.' Yet the middle-class family model was insistently portrayed as the norm, and consequently the justification for intervention in private lives. With the social order apparently in crisis and the crisis in the family at its root, reformers attempted to regain control of the population, encouraging and even demanding regulatory legislation and the expansion of public institutions to that end. They advocated public involvement in what was historically considered – and continued to be glorified as – the strictly private lives of families. Mental hospitals, school systems, reformatories, and penitentiaries became publicly controlled bodies under the administration of emergent experts in health and welfare. Despite the heightened clamouring for state action, its actual level remained limited during these years. But the forays that were made, and the insistence that the state be the prime countervailing force to family crisis and social degeneration, signified a noteworthy move away from the customary regulation by church and community towards state regulation. By 1914, governments at the municipal, provincial, and federal levels were enlarging their bureaucracies, and slowly assuming responsibility for a variety of services on behalf of the family that were historically private obligations and charitable duties. After the Great War, these steps would be consolidated.

PART II
A NEW DAY FOR FAMILIES:
MODERNIZING DOMESTICITY, 1914–1930

3

War and Reconstruction:
'Normalcy' and Its Discontents

When it began in August 1914, the Great War offered Canadians little sense that it was a 'turning point.' Because of a severe pre-war recession, many of the initial volunteers for overseas service were motivated not only by patriotism, but by the prospect of regular earnings. About 68,000 Canadian men would never see their homes again. Other disasters forced upwards the numbers of stricken families during the war years. In December 1917, more than two square kilometres of Halifax's north end were blown away after a French ship carrying explosives detonated in its harbour. Sixteen hundred died, mostly in the working-class neighbourhoods nearest the harbour. An additional 9,000 of the city's population of 50,000 were injured, and countless others were left homeless, widowed, orphaned. Finally, an international outbreak of Spanish influenza in the winter of 1918–19 killed almost as many Canadians as were lost on the Western front. Most of the 'flu' victims were between the ages of twenty and forty, crucial years of family formation.

This 'war to end all wars' also appeared to end much that was considered 'Victorian' or 'traditional.' It called into question society's confidence in never-ending progress, shaking the long-held conviction that God's purpose was realized in continuing human achievement. Temporarily, but acutely, the Great War shook the balance that some families had managed to recover as industrialization affected both their collective material basis and their individual lives as family members. This chapter outlines the impact of war-related structural and attitudinal changes on family roles and relations. The tone of contemporary public debates on the family testifies to the sense of urgency that prevailed. The war emergency brought women into public roles as never before, culminating in their political enfranchisement. At the same time that it opened these doors, it enhanced their maternal roles, both in private homes and as 'mothers of the race.' 'The family' acquired new significance in view of the depleted 'human stock' of an underpopulated young nation. The much-heralded return to 'normalcy' at war's end, consequently, would hinge upon a regenerated family that, for all its modern trappings, preserved intact its 'traditional' hierarchy defined by gender and age.

'Doing Your Bit': War, Society, and Family

The conduct of this 'war to end all wars' demanded all-out industrial participation, accelerating pre-war trends towards mechanization and the various deskilling, rationalizing, and 'speeding-up' processes that accompanied it under the name 'scientific management.' By the end of 1915, war contracts and recruitment sparked a rise in employment that would become a labour shortage the following year. The resulting higher wages for the still-predominantly male labour force did not keep pace with the steadily rising cost of living, however. In November 1918, an average weekly budget for a family of five was $13.49, compared with $7.96 at the outbreak of war in 1914. Loss of male breadwinners to enlistment, and the consequent 'manpower' shortage, drew more women into business and industrial employment. Many of them entered non-traditional sectors in munitions work, at least 'for the duration,' although they still earned from 50 to 80 per cent less than men in equivalent work. By the war's end more than 35,000 women, about 20 per cent of whom were married, were employed in munitions. Family-centred reform campaigns and 'home front' programs also drew more women into public participation than ever before.

The war effort necessitated the creation of a 'home front' as a supportive framework for industrial and military offensives. Responding to the 'call to arms,' voluntarist organizations attended to the social needs that the federal government was not prepared to address, preoccupied as it was with the conduct of the war, and largely suspicious of welfare intervention. Women's groups were particularly concerned about the situation of soldiers and the families soldiers left behind. To ensure their continued contact, women set up an information division of the Canadian Red Cross Society as an auxiliary to the Army Medical Corps. They established Maple Leaf Clubs to provide healthy recreation and companionship for soldiers on leave. Women and children, through such groups as the Women's Institutes and the Imperial Order Daughters of the Empire, knitted, sewed, packed parcels, served meals, held dances, and did Red Cross work. To maintain critical agricultural production while men enlisted, many women took over management of family farms, while others volunteered as farm labour. As Soldiers of the Soil, children also filled in for farmers' sons and hired hands who had gone to war. Some Aboriginal farm families in Southern Ontario began to cultivate previously fallow reserve lands to meet the urgent need, with much of the work going to women and children as men enlisted or worked in war industries.

Domestic budgets were seriously strained by wartime inflation, shortages, and the absence of male breadwinners, sparking much interest in the family economy among organized women. Affiliated with the National Council of Women, the Housewives Leagues called for government regulation of prices, standardization of sizes in manufactured goods, control over local food production and distribution, and the formation of cooperatives. The federal government also appointed Fuel and Food Controllers in 1917. They monitored distribution, enforced rationing where necessary, promoted home production and the use of alternatives, and worked to prevent panic and hoarding among consumers. Although labour and women's groups wanted action on the rising cost of living, the new Canada Food Board (1918) emphasized conserving food and increasing production for overseas export. To maximize production and mitigate dissent, the Anti-Loafing Law of 1918 commanded that all males between the ages of sixteen and sixty years be usefully employed. Each province mounted Vacant Lot Garden clubs to encourage vegetable and fruit growing, 'Keep a Hog' campaigns, and promotional activities based on such slogans as 'Eat Fish as a Patriotic Duty.' Housewives were naturally the primary focus of these efforts, as well as major participants.

The Canadian Patriotic Fund, incorporated by Parliament in August 1914, was the war's most important family-welfare initiative. Aiming 'to preserve the family's economic status in comfort and decency as a partial recognition of the services of the soldiers overseas,' it administered cash allowances through volunteer local committees directed by an Ottawa office. Fund-workers set up small cooperatives to sell food and fuel to recipients at cost. They also found domestic work for mothers, arranged housing, and provided medical care for children and donations of clothing and furniture. The assistance was certainly important to these families, but it was not without strings. Mostly middle-class women, the volunteers worked out appropriately thrifty household budgets, and visited periodically to keep an eye on housekeeping, spending, the mother's morality, and the cleanliness and courtesy of the children. Regulations were stringently enforced. Boarding with a soldier's family in the Montreal working-class neighbourhood of Griffintown, a young man was unable to persuade his landlady to install a telephone, even at his expense: the Fund expressly forbade telephones and she feared 'losing something.' Prominent Fund administrators such as Helen Reid argued that its regulatory functions were as important as its financial ones: 'the homes so sadly broken as a consequence of war have to be doubly safeguarded if the nation is to maintain its civilized standards.' Increases in such symptoms of family crisis as infant mortality, juvenile delinquency, and divorce underscored 'the need for patriotic home service.' When it became evident that charity was an inadequate response to the soldiers' sacrifices, and the job too big even for dedicated volunteers, the federal government took over the administration of widows' and dependants' pensions. The 'home inspection' aspects continued as before.

The war emergency also brought the realization of several long-sought maternal feminist causes: prohibition, suffrage, and mothers' allowances. Dedicated suffragist and popular writer Nellie McClung explained that the 'liquor traffic' had 'waged war on women and children all down the centuries.' Fearing the corruption of husbands, fathers, and sons overseas, women used patriotism, sacrifice, and appeals to personal morality and family values to urge prohibition. Between 1915 and 1916 every province except Quebec went 'dry.' In December 1917, the newly elected coalition federal government announced total prohibition of the manufacture, importation, and transport of any beverage of more than 2.5 per cent alcohol. In the heady atmosphere of war, prohibition symbolized a major step towards regenerated family values and social mores. After years of debate and much petitioning by women's organizations, Manitoba became the first province to legislate mothers' allowances in 1916. With the exception of Quebec, the other provinces quickly followed suit to provide state assistance to widows with more than one child. Women's obvious 'home front' commitment to duty – and their political value in support of men's duty – also convinced Sir Robert Borden's Union government that their enfranchisement could no longer be postponed. The Wartime Elections Act of 1917 gave the vote to the wives, widows, mothers, sisters, and daughters of soldiers to salute their special sacrifice. All female British subjects twenty-one years and over were ultimately enfranchised in the Women's Franchise Act of 1918.

Returning to 'Normalcy': Postwar Disequilibrium

Just over 650,000 Canadians served in the armed forces. About 68,000 lost their lives, and approximately as many suffered physical and mental wounds that made the resumption of pre-war lives difficult or impossible. Their experiences in the trenches marked this 'lost generation' of men profoundly. Survivors re-entered a vastly changed society, reuniting with parents and siblings, wives and children, whose lives did not stand still in their absence. Although more professional and 'scientific' than ever, medicine, psychology, and related social services were ill-prepared to ease their civilian readjustment. Many wives and children had to cope with shell-shocked and physically and emotionally damaged men in a time when community facilities, prostheses, transportation devices, reconstructive surgery, and physical and psychotherapy were either unavailable or too primitive to fix what was broken. Some men retreated into their own worlds or took to drinking for comfort, becoming, as one veteran described them, 'what you call old soldiers, old bums ... they just went to pieces.' A girl who was thirteen years old when her wounded father returned to their prairie home in 1919 could not remember 'one day when he wasn't drunk' until she left five years later.

To ensure that Canada was 'a home fit for heroes,' the Department of Soldiers Civil Re-establishment attempted to provide for veterans in a just and equitable manner. The results were mostly dismal. About 25,000 veterans took advantage of a government colonization scheme to marry and settle, or resettle families, on homesteads. Land grants in undeveloped territory, largely in the northern reaches of Ontario and Quebec, and on the prairies, and a year's paid training in farming techniques, did not make up for the fact that the land was often unyielding and many more provisions were needed than those supplied. In the words of a veteran's wife, participating families endured 'another war of poverty and hunger and cold.' Six Nations veterans, who had formed two complete companies in the 114th Battalion and were among the first Canadians to encounter gas warfare in France, were much disturbed by the act's application. The federal government now claimed authority over reserve land, an infringement of the chiefs' customary right to allot land. Like many veterans, they were dissatisfied with what they could only interpret as lack of public appreciation for their sacrifice, especially since their families had long suffered from discriminatory government policies and society's prejudice. It quickly became apparent to Native families across the nation that their position would not improve substantially through any 'reconstruction' projects.

War and its after-effects thus sparked much discontent. Anti-labour wartime legislation, conscription, and the government's failure to address the continuing postwar problems of unemployment, high inflation, and the status of veterans, aggravated labour unrest. The climax came in 1919, a year marked by the famous Winnipeg General Strike, and an outflow of supportive labour protest that manifested itself across the nation. In the West and the Maritimes, farmers organized to protest against an increasingly urban, industrial, central Canadian politics that neglected their particular needs. By 1920, the Progressive movement had united enough disgruntled Canadians to win significant parliamentary representation. The war-related grievances of Quebec residents also disrupted the peace. Fuelled by Anglo-Canadian disdain for the voluntary enlistment efforts of the Québécois, who were accused of not upholding Canada's commitment to Great Britain, the Conscription Crisis of 1917 created a lasting national divide between the two Canadas. Moreover, the nation's increasing urbanization, reflected in the majority urban population measured for the first time in the census of 1921, appeared a special threat to Quebec's distinctiveness. According to the Church and the social elite, cities weakened the francophone Catholic family's attachment to the 'true vocation' and the 'purer' society of the countryside. The result of such pressures was a cultural nationalism that celebrated the interdependence of family, religion, language, and rural vocation.

Despite the decade's historic image as the 'Roaring Twenties' and the 'Jazz Age,' many Canadians did not take part in the implied festivities of the 1920s. At decade's end, only 143,600 Canadians, fewer than 5 per cent of all income earners, garnered the $2,500 necessary to be taxed under the federal income tax legislation introduced during the war. The average annual wage in 1929 was $1,200. The Department of Labour's own budget estimated that maintaining an 'average' Canadian family – two adults and three children under the age of twelve years – at a minimum standard of health and decency required an annual income of $1,430. Sixty-nine per cent of men and 82 per cent of working women earned less than $1,000 per year. Not surprisingly, contemporary surveys of Halifax, Montreal, Winnipeg, and Vancouver showed little evidence of any real improvement in the material condition of many working-class families.

Well might fearful middle-class Canadians believe that the nation was on the road to perdition. Unsettled conditions such as these, intensified by public exhaustion with the war, fostered impatience to return to 'normalcy,' a term attributed to American president Warren G. Harding. The result was a defensive backlash that focused more emphatically than ever on rescuing 'the family besieged.' All foreboding to the contrary, however, the family was proving resilient. Although the divorce rate began to rise in the last year of the war, continuing a slow upward climb through the next two decades, the actual number of divorced Canadians was minute. The 1921 census revealed more married Canadians than at any previous time on record. Three-quarters of Canadian women were married by age thirty-four, and over 90 per cent of all women and 91 per cent of all men eventually married. Couples also appeared to be marrying earlier, reversing the upward trend that had begun in the mid-nineteenth-century. In 1901, men married at an average age of twenty-eight years, women at twenty-six years. The average age at marriage in 1921 was twenty-seven years for men and twenty-four years for women.

In contrast to the high marriage rate, the birth rate continued to fall: from 29.3 per thousand in 1921 to 23.5 in 1929. The modern Canadian family now averaged three children instead of the customary five or six. By the 1920s it was less common for women over thirty to give birth, a pattern typically found when marital fertility declines. Fertility was markedly lower in towns and cities than in rural areas. Those of British origin had a lower total fertility rate than those of other European origins. Educated women had fewer children than those with less education. The average Ontario household in 1931, with 4.2 persons, was smaller than the national average; with 5.32 persons, the average Quebec household was somewhat larger. The pre-war worries about 'race suicide,' which the worriers defined as the decline of the 'better stock' of white Anglo-Celtic Protestants, were fuelled anew by these statistics, especially in light of war casualties.

The Shape of Things to Come: Modern Trends

Perhaps the most significant modern trend, in what it seemed to forecast for 'the family,' was the changing role, appearance, and attitude of 'the girl of the new day.' Social critics were alarmed by the 'flapper,' the 'new woman' who was attempting to fly the nest, or so it was feared. Armed with the vote, more formal schooling than her mother, new access to jobs, and new ideas about her 'proper sphere,' the flapper appeared a singular threat to middle-class domestic ideals. Young unmarried women were now more likely to work in the company of men, often in the lower-level office, sales, and service jobs that were becoming both more available and more feminized. They were also adopting a simplified modern uniform: the overall look was somewhat androgynous, with hair cut short or 'bobbed,' a slender boyish form replacing the large-breasted, wide-hipped, maternal feminine ideal of the Victorian age. Women who adopted the style, as well as the 'manly' habits of public smoking and drinking, set off all sorts of warning bells about the decline of 'womanliness' and its corresponding domestic roles.

The modern woman, the modern look, and the modern age gave rise to a perceived 'revolution in morals' which clearly did not bode well for the family. For some, the war had exposed middle-class attitudes about sexuality as sham and hypocrisy. 'Waiting' for marriage seemed ridiculous to young people who saw how quickly plans could shatter and 'forever' be destroyed. The 'new morality' was also greatly influenced by mass culture. The growing importance of movies, advertising, and mass-circulation magazines, many of them American, helped to create the aura of a new day that was slamming the door irrevocably on outmoded tradition. By creating such modern cultural icons as the Sheik – a smouldering Rudolph Valentino – and the Vamp – a seductive Theda Bara – Hollywood was demolishing middle-class, Anglo-Celtic ideals about manliness, femininity, and 'respectable' sexuality.

The pre-war social-purity crusade was an ironic force behind this new morality. Enlisting countless social reformers and the 'helping professions,' this conservative campaign had actually broken through resistant Victorian taboos concerning public discussion of sexuality. Canadian medicine and psychology grudgingly acknowledged women's sexuality, just as Sigmund Freud's recognition of the centrality of the sexual impulse to all humanity began to make headway among educated North Americans. But if modern women were permitted a sexual nature, it was still not equivalent to that of men except in 'unnatural' women; it was still carefully regulated within heterosexual relations sanctified by marriage; it was still grounded in residual Victorian notions about superior feminine self-control, hence feminine virtue and deportment. Above all, it was still oriented towards motherhood.

The 1920s introduced new courtship patterns, virtually eliminating the traditional form whereby the man 'called' on the young woman, usually in the family home and under familial supervision. The new 'dating' generally required 'going out,' often in groups of young people, often entailing commercial amusements such as movies and dances, and

usually without adult chaperones. Dating also implied a fairly
frequent turnover of partners before the 'going steady' commitment which was supposed to lead to marriage. Such an
active sampling, previously frowned upon as encouraging
promiscuity, was now considered essential by young people
with new notions about romantic partnerships and 'companionate' marriages. It is impossible to know whether premarital sex was actually increasing as a result of these shifts in
attitudes and behaviour among the younger generation. In
all likelihood, unmarried couples engaging in sexual relations were probably following the historic pattern of doing
so within the bounds of certain traditional assumptions. For
immigrant, working-class, and rural couples, sex usually took
place in romantic relationships and, at least from the woman's point of view, under a promise of marriage. Regardless
of class or ethnic background, loss of 'reputation,' with or
without pregnancy, brought dishonour to women and their
families. If views on the gravity of the 'sin' differed slightly,
no organized religion tolerated sex outside marriage. In the
years between the wars, Montreal's Hôpital de la Miséricorde
admitted at least 560 unwed mothers annually, evidence of
the penalty that women continued to pay in the absence of
effective and accessible contraception. The measures taken
to hide a premarital pregnancy required leaving home, en-
tering an institution, changing one's name, relinquishing the
infant for adoption – all consequences of what was still regarded as scandal, sin, the woman's fitting punishment, and
reason enough to abstain before marriage.

**Mr and Mrs Consumer and Family:
The Modern Household**

The coming of peace hardly signalled a return to 'normalcy,'
so pervasive was the sense of change in the immediate aftermath of war. The world of family, church, small town, and
rural village, already rudely shaken by pre-war changes, could
not be re-established. The balance between the family as unit
of production and the family as unit of consumption contin-

ued to shift towards the latter. The middle-class housewife of the 1920s was more than ever a manager of consumption. Working-class and farm women, too, were buying rather than producing a larger portion of their families' everyday needs, particularly food and clothing. If they were becoming more affordable, many of the new household products and appliances were still priced beyond the reach of many Canadian families. In the unstable economic environment of the early 1920s, continued high prices and unemployment tended to postpone the purchase of even the coveted family home. Tom Moore, leader of the country's major labour federation, the Trades and Labor Congress, echoed the feelings of many postwar workers in remarking that 'everything seems against the young fellow with domestic ideas.'

Rather than continue to represent the family as a refuge in a morally corrupt world, the family experts of the day designed a new, improved 'modern' family that they hoped would better withstand the dangers posed by modernity. Fundamental to the ideal modern family were its middle-class grounding, its gendered role definitions, and its adoption by English- or French-speaking Canadians for specific cultural ends. No longer depicted principally as a sacred and civil duty, a moral 'container' for sexuality and procreation, marriage became a celebration of romantic, emotional, and sexual fulfilment. Weddings became much more lavish, carefully scripted social affairs, featuring special attire, floral bouquets, an entourage of bridesmaids and ushers to attend the happy couple, receptions for family and friends, and much emphasis on the wedding trip, or honeymoon. The new model of companionate marriage made husband and wife a romantic couple, best friends and partners in the enterprise of family. A mutually fulfilling sex life was the new ideal, a far cry, at least in principle, from the Victorian notion that women 'tolerated' sex purely to answer to their maternal calling. How much this was actually realized by married couples remains speculative, but it is significant that sex was now depicted as an important part of a healthy, happy marital relationship, and not solely as the means to procreation. Just as the modern marriage was based on the notion of shared rights and responsibilities, relations between parents and children were likewise expected to be more intimate and openly affectionate. Parents were not just guardians and providers; they were also supposed to be companions, 'pals' to their children, and exemplary role-models for appropriate gender and social relations. Properly raised children would cooperate with their model parents to maintain family harmony, but also in the national interest. They were 'citizens in the making.'

For working-class couples setting up new households in the 1920s, 'home' meant much more than the cheap lodgings that many of them had grown up in. Poverty, hard work, and the expectation of marriage continued to shape their life-course, but their aspirations for something better distinguished this generation from that of its parents. Getting 'something better' was contingent upon smaller families, a family wage, improved health, a comfortable house, and a less-wearing round of daily tasks. A developing agenda of public health and social welfare, and an economy increasingly focused on domesticity and household consumption, made the dream at least appear worth dreaming. By 1928 it was, for the first time, theoretically possible for the average male industrial worker to earn sufficient wages to provide for a family on his own – providing that he was employed the entire course of the year, that he had three or fewer children, and that no serious illness or accident befell his dependants. If the male-breadwinner ideal was consolidated in the 1920s, its realization remained only a little less problematic than it had at the turn of the century. Until the Second World War years, only a minority actually achieved it. Ideas about companionate marriage and the male-breadwinner family were making inroads into the working class, but they remained necessarily more flexible concepts in families where material conditions often determined domestic roles and relations. Organized labour used the ideal to argue that male heads of families were entitled to the 'family wage' that would allow them to carry out their manly roles as providers.

With the expansion of the consumer economy, home and family were increasingly connected with the physical residence. Businesses began making explicit appeals to the ideal modern family, playing no small part in its social construction, and specifically in its gender constructions. Mass culture emphasized newness, sensation, and style. All of these were subject to manipulation by producers and advertisers, who used the sparkling new technology of radio and 'talking' film to sell both goods and images. Advertising, the engine of consumerism, represented housewives as 'queens of the hearth,' men as successful providers, and healthy, well-adjusted children whose welfare was guaranteed by particular products and services. The sellers helped to create a culture of expectation for the panoply of consumer products made possible by technological innovation, mass production, the development of department and grocery store chains, consumer credit and instalment buying. Mechanical refrigerators, electric ranges, telephones, radios, and automobiles were depicted as the 'modern conveniences' without which Canadian families were clearly deprived, and obviously not modern. Marketing experts were naturally keen to court women, who traditionally managed household finances.

Until the start of the Great Depression, consumer expenditures rose steadily. The immediate postwar years saw the establishment of department and supermarket chain stores: Kresge's, Safeway's, Red and White, Loblaw's, Woodward's, Tamblyn's, Woolworth's, and Dominion, pushed into the marketplace long reigned over by small family shops and the established Eaton's department stores, also a family enterprise. National brands in staples, foods, and appliances offered more buying selection, while making shopping for the family a relatively standardized experience across the country, at least in towns and cities. Catalogues from Eaton's, circulating since 1883, presented a broadening array of the same tantalizing wares to isolated and rural families across the nation. Taste, style, fashion, and fun began to modify their local, regional, cultural, and class components, becoming subject to what was deemed to be 'it' in European and North American style centres such as New York, Hollywood, Paris, London – and, for Canadians at least, Toronto and Montreal.

Working-class families opting for home ownership, usually after years of renting and saving, often began with a 'starter' home to add on to and remodel as the family's fortunes, and perhaps the family itself, expanded. As transportation improved, city limits stretched and farm land was developed, suburban living became more feasible. Many purchased lots and built their own 'starters' with the assistance of kin and friends. These were frequently one-storey bungalows with partial basements, often without indoor bathrooms. Arriving just before the outbreak of war, a Scottish family with four children lived for many years in a four-room bungalow that their father and his friends 'threw up' in Grandview, British Columbia. Their own labour and ingenuity gradually transformed the original three-room frame cottage of another family into a two-storey home with a bathroom and three bedrooms, although it still lacked running water in the early 1920s. Such 'starters' and their later versions prevailed in working-class neighbourhoods in Vancouver, Toronto, and Halifax, as well as smaller urban centres.

Middle-class families generally went through fewer stages to establish the 'family home.' The prevalent style of middle-class homes across Canada by the start of the First World War was the 1 1/2- or 2-storey house with a gable facing the street, a ground-floor porch, and an off-centre entrance door that usually opened into a narrow foyer. There were typically separate living and dining rooms and a kitchen on the main floor, three bedrooms and a bathroom upstairs. Houses of this kind, and the equally common 'foursquare' which first appeared around 1910, were made available to the masses through pattern-books and builders' catalogues, often pre-cut or prefabricated. The 1919 Eaton's catalogue featured a dozen 'foursquares' with pre-cut components requiring on-site assembly.

Also catering to the new identification of the ideal family

with its living space were entire 'matched suites' of furniture for each specific room, in a newly modern spare design that promoted comfort (for the tired breadwinner) and ease of upkeep (for the careful housewife) over 'traditional' Victorian clutter and fussiness. A flourishing selection of special wallpapers, furnishings, and gender-appropriate decorative accessories for children's rooms similarly reflected this emphasis on the cosy, cheery, comfortable family home as the key to domestic happiness. Home design was reorienting the house to the backyard, which became an extension of the home for the private recreation of middle-class families. Porch-sitting, street-play, and chatting with neighbours came to be hallmarks of older working-class and immigrant communities, not-quite-respectable emblems of more 'traditional' patterns of sociability.

Postwar family life was strongly influenced by the rise of mass culture and its ethic of consumption, as represented by radio, 'movies,' mass-produced musical recordings, and commercialized entertainments. These developments tended to blur class lines and weaken a distinctively class-based culture, as did the growing ethnic, racial, and gender mix within the Canadian working class. In some ways, class and community solidarity were redirected to the private family. The radio was an important source of family entertainment, especially on the prairies, where so many lived far from kin, neighbours, and commercial recreation facilities. No longer were theatre, opera, and sports events limited by local talent and accessibility: radio could broadcast musical symphonies and hockey games from across the country. When Henry Ford revolutionized production by introducing the assembly line at his automobile plants in 1914, he also brought the 'family car' within the realm of possibility for unprecedented numbers of buyers. Ownership more than doubled between 1920 and 1930, when one in nine Canadians owned cars. Outings, even to see performances and games in other towns, were much more readily accomplished than in the days of bus and train travel. Advertisers took advantage of this powerful symbol of modern technology to sell not only cars, but also cosy domestic images of 'Sunday drives' and 'family holidays.'

Because of the decline of domestic service, only one in twenty middle-class housewives had regular paid help in 1921, by comparison to approximately one in five in the 1860s. The 'servant problem' and the vogue for scientific management and 'efficiency' persuaded builders to design layouts tailored to the clients' specific domestic needs. Although the designers, builders, and house-buyers were men, women actively influenced the physical structure of modern homes. But modern as they might have been, their arrangement still reflected the traditional gendered division of domestic labour. The kitchen remained the 'woman's room,' even if displaying modern sensibilities in style and components. Model kitchens minimized wasted effort and physical movement, placing sink, stove, refrigerator, cupboards, and drawers within the busy housewife's easy reach. Gas stoves first appeared in 1919, electric refrigerators in 1920. Hot-water and warm-air heating systems, enamelled bathtubs and flush toilets, the replacement of gas-lighting with electricity, and the increasing affordability of telephones and radios did much to support the ideal of the private family in its cosy home, independent from neighbours and protected against the outside world. The long-term effects of modern domestic science and technology were elevated standards of hygiene and comfort, but also elevated expectations of women. Reduced physical labour, therefore, did not necessarily mean less housework. For many women, it simply meant the reordering of an intensive workday. By the mid-1920s, the time spent by urban housewives preparing meals, making clothes, and preserving and canning foods had declined from six hours daily to three. Meanwhile, the amount devoted to cleaning and child care rose sharply to fill the time that had been freed.

Modifying the Modern: Domestic Continuities

Despite the postwar rhetoric of modernity, much remained

of previous incarnations of the domestic ideal. The male-breadwinner concept increasingly dear to middle-class hearts was proving ever more captivating to the working class. The new romantic emphasis on heterosexual love also encouraged more rigid definitions of the norm, making same-sex relations appear all the more deviant. The notion of heterosexual marriage as the only publicly sanctioned, therefore 'normal,' setting for sexuality was never endangered. The Victorian ideal of mother as the virtuous and self-sacrificing 'angel in the house' became the ideal of mother as scientific home manager, a change in style more than substance. The home as 'haven' was now a clean, smoothly running, efficient modern factory. If they were more equitable in principle, the internal relations of the modern family continued to be fundamentally ordered by gender and age, with the usual class, regional, and ethnic variations.

The gender constructions that determined the sexual division of labour, models of masculinity and femininity, and 'proper' behaviour, continued to be important to working-class notions of respectability. For men, the job traditionally defined manliness through masculine skill and physical strength, as well as rate of pay. Changes in production, with growing division of labour and assembly-line methods, meant that fewer male workers could identify themselves by skill and strength alone. The qualifications of 'manliness' refocused on the ability of the male head of household to provide for his family by himself. For working-class women, respectability was both a source of identity and a crucial skill in itself. The respectable housewife, with her impeccable house, refined domestic skills, and well-behaved children, became the icon of the age, as advertisers directed their modern wares at her. This seemingly classless domestic figure dominated media, social policy, and. to some degree, feminist discussions about women's position in modern society. Such a construction of their modern role appealed to many working-class women, faced with limited opportunities for the education and employment that allowed the new 'career woman' both a measure of independence and public status. Low-paid, gender-typed employment removed them from any possibility of a 'family wage.' Material conditions and ideology thus sustained each other in the construction of working-class gender identities and domestic roles.

Even as agriculture was increasingly mechanized, farmers continued to depend on the labour of wives and children. Rural electrification was a key election pledge during the heydey of the Progressive movement in the 1920s, though in some provinces, such as Quebec, fewer than 20 per cent of farms had electricity as late as the 1940s. Cars, telephones, and radios were slowly becoming more common. In such popular farm journals as *The Grain Growers' Guide* and *The Family Herald*, updated images of the farm family brought it closer to the modern urban ideal. The modern farm man was portrayed as a successful producer and businessman, a good husband and good farmer who secured a healthy family environment by 'providing' well through efficient business methods. Husband and wife were depicted as partners in running the farm, but the wife was left to manage her own domestic department. While they continued to perform important productive functions, by the 1920s farm women were purchasing approximately three-quarters of all products for the home.

The 1920s were a time of great change for Northern Inuit families, which had remained relatively untouched by Euro-Canadian ways due to the lateness of white settlement and active trade in the North. The Roman Catholic Church and the Hudson's Bay Company established permanent posts on the south side of Chesterfield Inlet in Caribou Inuit country in the summer of 1912. Over the next two decades, tiny Euro-Canadian settlements sprang up at scattered points across Southern Keewatin. Inuit families managed to maintain their cultural separateness and traditional domestic relations during the early years, as missionaries established their schools and attempted their conversions. The Great Famine, which began in 1915, shattered this independence. By 1925, the

Inuit in the area had been reduced to 500 from the original 1,500 barely a decade earlier. As the survivors took on the 'white man's' socio-economic organization and its corresponding settlement lifestyle, families became larger, and women's confinement to domestic work increased along with their actual domestic labour.

Aboriginal families also felt the impact of increasing urbanization. The pull of the city, and better transportation, drew men out of subsistence farming on the reserves into industrial labour. Many commuted to manufacturing, construction, and railway jobs, returning only on weekends, leaving the household and any agricultural production in the charge of wives and children. When the traditional economy of the northern Ojibwa of Ontario was seriously undermined by overtrapping and declining prices, some men found jobs with the railways, lumber camps, and mills. Families that moved to scattered settlements along these railways and close to the mills experienced profound disruption. Life for the 'line Indians,' in close proximity to a predominantly male population of transient non-Aboriginals, destroyed familiar domestic and community patterns that had evolved from the earlier difficult adjustment to reserve life. Contemporary studies showed that these relocated families often experienced apathy and aimlessness, with corresponding increases in alcohol abuse, domestic violence, and family breakdown.

The family remained the principal agency of socialization and transmitter of culture to Aboriginal children, but it was harshly affected by the expanding residential-school system and the decline in importance of the extended family. As the nuclear family became more self-enclosed, Aboriginal children often lost opportunity for the intimate contact with kin, especially their elders, the traditional core of their social relations. In order for children to make their way in modern Canada, the knowledge of the elders had to be relinquished in favour of the knowledge imparted by schools and other Euro-Canadian institutions, such as public health departments, family courts, and social service agencies. If many parents accepted that this was their children's only hope for a better life, their compliance was hard-won and never complete. Many upheld their traditional ceremonies and healing rituals despite attending Catholic or Protestant churches and using 'white' medical doctors. But the overall effects of change on Aboriginal families in the 1920s continued to be negative.

For various immigrant groups, the postwar years featured family resettlement, as sojourning collapsed with the outbreak of war. The time that elapsed between the sojourner's arrival and that of his wife and children naturally created a discrepancy in their rates of acculturation and adaptation. By this time, most men probably had a working knowledge of the language, and a sense of 'Canadian' customs, which would assist their newly arrived families, but might also make them feel 'alien' in regards to each other. Accustomed to managing for their families in the husband's absence, wives may have been reluctant to resume submissive roles, especially in a country where women were reputedly more independent than in the Old World. In families settled before the war, generational tensions probably increased as parents maintained their attachment to Old World ways while children had little personal memory of them, and wanted above all to 'fit in' with their peers and as Canadians. Needless to say, flappers and their male counterparts caused much consternation in homes of immigrants with strong religious backgrounds and steadfast devotion to the concept of filial obedience. The demeanour and behaviour of daughters, whose personal morality represented familial honour and reputation, were a special concern. An Italian-born Montreal girl, already working ten hours a day in a macaroni factory at the age of thirteen, complained that all she seemed to do was 'eat, work and sleep ... it was a fight every time I wanted to go out.' She and her sisters were occasionally permitted to attend a movie – always chaperoned by other family members – but never a dance.

By the end of the Great War, the abundant and varied diversions of the new age, the dance halls, cinemas, spectator sports, automobile trips, and 'speakeasies,' were energizing

a youth culture that would come to signify mass culture itself. It appeared to contemporaries that 'the idea with lots
of the youth of today is what's the use of staying home if
there's anywhere else you can go?' While regular church attendance drew 'scarcely half our people,' lamented a con-
tributor to *Saturday Night* magazine, over 90 per cent of
Canadians were evidently regular movie-goers, and fully 60
per cent of these were under the age of eighteen. In the 1920s
middle-class adolescents were likely to attend high school;
participate in the burgeoning 'extracurriculum' of athletics,
clubs, sororities, and fraternities; and take part in dances and
parties. For all classes, increasing amounts of time were spent
away from family and in the company of the newly important
peer group. 'Everybody was so repressed through the war that
we all just went nuts,' recalled one man about his 'coming of
age' in the 1920s. A woman, in high school at the time, remembered a lot of 'horseplay' between girls who were more
'permissive' and boys who were 'more daring.' A candid account by three adolescent girls in *Maclean's* magazine in 1922
casually detailed the popularity of 'fussing parties,' evidently
involving 'just jazz and lovemaking,' along with smoking and
drinking. As young people became a stronger market force,
able to command the goods and services that suited them,
the public perception of adolescence as a distinct stage of life
with its own unique culture was also enhanced.

While working-class children were staying in school longer
and participating in new pastimes as well, the prolonged
dependence and insulated character of modern adolescence
were beyond family means for many of them. Forty-two per
cent of fifteen- to nineteen-year-olds in Edmonton were earn-
ing wages in 1921. Their class position and contributory role
in the family economy obliged many adolescents to choose
wage labour over learning. A fourteen-year-old girl employed
as a stenographer 'in one of the biggest factories in Orillia [,
Ontario]' did typing, shorthand, and dictaphone transcrip-
tion, despite her youth. Another of the same age, with the
help of two sisters, ran a telegraph office from her family's
farm on the Gaspé, while also attending school. If their fi-

nancial contributions were still needed, fewer working-class families expected working children to hand over their entire paycheques. They were required to pay board, and likely most of their own support, but they appear to have retained some 'pocket money' to permit them a measure of involvement in the emergent popular culture that their middle-class peers were making their own.

At the other end of the life-course, the condition of the elderly reached a crisis point during the 1920s. The historic vulnerability of the old became more pronounced with the rising cost of living and economic fluctuations that made keeping jobs increasingly difficult for older men, among the first to be laid off. The prospects for elderly women, especially widows, were as dismal as ever. The Nova Scotia Commission on Old Age Pensions of 1928–30 noted that, in every jurisdiction surveyed, the majority had an annual income less than $200. An 'alarming' number – more than one-third – reported having no income at all. In most cases, children remained the major source of financial assistance. The proportions were highest in Saskatchewan, Alberta, British Columbia, and Nova Scotia, perhaps suggesting less opportunity for the elderly to continue independent living in these provinces. Those without the support of children were obliged to turn to charity, and even to illegal activities. A Halifax man, a former boilermaker and ironworker, sixty-four years old and disabled, was arrested for running a gaming house to earn his keep and avoid the poorhouse. Even direct state involvement did little to improve the lot of the elderly. The federal Old Age Pensions Act of 1927 was a shared-cost program that most provinces could not afford to enter until the 1930s. Many would do so at that time of economic collapse because it was a way to transfer costs for the burgeoning relief of the unemployed back into federal hands.

Conclusion

In the years from 1914 to 1930, marriage and family formation remained the choice of most Canadians, but definite changes were making themselves felt. The contraction in family size testifies to the steady spread of birth control despite the continued illegality of all mechanical means of contraception. It also indicates the growing correlation of small families with a better quality of family life. Infant and child mortality remained high, but improvements were being made through public education campaigns and expanded public health and sanitation measures, especially mass immunization and milk inspection. Longer life expectancy also increased the average length of marriages. Combined with smaller family size, this development extended the time between children leaving home and the death of husband or wife. Couples who married in 1920, therefore, could expect this post-parental stage of the life-course to be almost seven years longer than it was for those who married in 1900, a demographic fact with important implications for both the marital relationship and old age. Adolescence also acquired clearer boundaries in the 1920s, as the age of school-leaving was raised to sixteen years in most provinces, making high school the new marker of that life-stage for more young Canadians.

If much of family life remained within bounds that we can recognize as holdovers from the pre-war years, the profound sociocultural impact of the war itself gave rise to challenges to earlier family models. Anxiety and a sense of loss led to nostalgic laments from press and pulpit, from reformers and family experts, for a 'traditional' family that had existed more in mythic form than in reality for many Canadians. The myth, however, was powerful, and obviously still meaningful, even for those who had never really experienced that form of family and its relations. Paradoxically, there was also a marked sense that traditionalism was the sort of evil that had led to global cataclysm. Consequently, social commentators argued, it was time to look forward, to be 'modern,' an appeal particularly strong for the young, who were more 'modern' than their parents could hope to be.

The central question of family-crisis discourses in the early

postwar years was whether 'the family' could possibly withstand any more modifications and still be recognizable in its
cherished patriarchal form. For many, the answer involved
getting governments to formulate policies that, while modern in the extent of state regulation that they promoted, were
intended to support and reinforce the patriarchal family of
tradition. A new generation of experts established itself as
guides and mentors in all family matters. With the help of
an expanding state, these experts concentrated on women
and children as the principal players on the modern domestic scene. As the social sciences were institutionalized and
professionalized, their methods of survey and analysis were
applied to the study of the family. The keywords of the period's family-centred reform campaigns were science, education, state regulation, professional expertise, and 'efficiency.'

4

New Model Families: Science and State Intervention

The Great War renewed calls upon the state to do something about the toll taken by modern industry and modern warfare, as witnessed in damaged health, 'broken' families, juvenile delinquency, and the prospects of social breakdown. The war's horrendous casualties also focused attention on the population as a biological resource, legitimizing arguments about state intervention to counter those losses through healthy families. Reformist and professional organizations, women's and labour groups, demanded the creation of special government agencies dedicated to assisting families, especially children, now regarded as precious 'national assets.' The most important of these government initiatives was the Canadian Council on Child Welfare, established in 1920. It became the Council on Child and Family Welfare in 1929, indicating the more-inclusive mandate which was the legacy of the decade's family-centred reform debates and measures. Attempts to establish a 'modern' family and a 'new domesticity' were integral parts of the postwar 'reconstruction,' as it was officially proclaimed.

This chapter considers the creation of a modern relationship among families, family experts, and the state. Science and technology, management and efficiency, imbued the relations of reproduction as well as those of production. The ideal modern home was a smoothly run factory, the ideal marriage a business partnership, the ideal housewife/mother a manager, the ideal child a 'little machine.' For a modern industrial nation, these domestic roles and relations were the best to which human beings could aspire. In the immediate postwar years, a new group of 'scientific' experts, often assisted by new state departments concerned with public welfare, purposefully studied and surveilled Canadian families to that end. As a result of their projects, the family became so closely associated with the state that, as historian James Snell remarks, 'to question its legitimacy was virtually tantamount to treason.'

Responding to Crisis: Familism, Maternalism, and Social Policy

The tone of postwar public debates about the family reflects the sense of emergency that prevailed. Revelations about the poor physical health of army recruits, and the ultimate toll of so many 'young men in their prime' and 'future fathers of the race,' magnified pre-war concerns about 'race suicide,' social degeneration, and the collapse of the patriarchal family. As the previous chapter indicated, the ideal family of the day, however 'modern' its depiction, was premised on traditional gender-defined social roles. Contradictory though it appears, therefore, the immediate postwar years witnessed both the rise of the 'flapper' and a veritable cult of motherhood. Maternalism became the central strategy of a politics of regeneration that would uplift both family and nation. The connections between motherhood and a widely defined national 'health' were repeated, circulated, and politicized across the land, with important effects for developing social policy.

The very women's organizations that had long fought to widen women's sphere promoted motherhood in its every idealized facet. The National Council of Women declared that a successful postwar reconstruction demanded 'a realization of the power of consecrated motherhood.' With prohibition collapsing by the mid-1920s, the Woman's Christian

Temperance Union tried to entice new members by arguing that 'the WCTU gives every woman in Canada a chance to help in the work of making our country a land of happy homes.' Organized labour women also called upon women's 'mighty power for the uplift of womanhood, the family and the home,' especially for the 'protection' of motherhood and childhood. Much like the Ontario-born Women's Institutes, which expanded through the prairies during the 1920s, the Cercles des fermières, formed in 1915 in the Chicoutimi region of Quebec, aimed to professionalize the housekeeping and childrearing skills of farm wives so that families would stay on the land and thrive. Canadian women, as well as men, responded to the challenges represented by suffrage, growing female labour-force participation, and the 'girl of the new day' by reaffirming the mutuality of the ideal home, family, and society.

Postwar reformist discourses focused on potential: science, technology, and a sanctified motherhood would join forces to give life to a shiny new world. This utopian vision was inspired by faith in modern science, but it was sustained by faith in traditional gender and family roles and commitment to the existing socio-economic system. Paradoxically, even if mothers so often appeared the root of family problems, reformers believed that they remained the family's one hope of adapting to modern conditions without disintegrating in the process. In Quebec, priests, physicians, and politicians supported pro-natalist campaigns, urging frequent childbearing as the most important duty of women to Catholic French Canada, which looked to its mothers for its survival. Parallel family-crisis arguments in English Canada also tied reproduction to national progress, so much so that Dr Helen MacMurchy, first chief of the federal Health Department's Division of Child Welfare (1920), could declare unequivocally that 'nations are built of babies.' Everyone understood the centrality of motherhood to the cause of national greatness.

The Great War impressed upon civic-minded Canadians their patriotic duty to save infants and keep them healthy in order to replace the young men who had left empty places, and the children who would now never be born. Haphazard, voluntarist efforts to lower infant mortality were not enough. In Quebec, infant mortality was still responsible for 12 to 17 per cent of all deaths in the province between 1900 and 1929. Montreal had one of the highest rates in the Western world. In 1924, the national rate was a worrisome 101 per 1,000 live births. The barely moving numbers suggested to doctors that they had to take a stronger leadership role in the campaign to save babies for Canada. What was needed was a scientific program directed by the medical profession and supported by the state. On the grounds of national health and productivity, the medical profession denigrated both traditional childcare methods and traditional advisers among kin and neighbours. As non-medical supporters picked up the medical discourse, then repeated and embellished it, motherhood was transformed into a 'science' and a 'profession of the highest order,' in deliberate contrast to the 'natural' and 'instinctive' relationship of tradition. When Dr Helen MacMurchy's 1928 *Report on Maternal Mortality* publicized the maternity-related deaths that annually claimed at least 1,500 women, the causes of infant and maternal welfare melded into one. The solutions proposed were educational, supervisory, and regulatory, focusing on 'scientific motherhood' as the best approach. Because notions about maternal ignorance respected no barriers of class or race, the experts had a potentially unlimited audience of women who needed their instruction simply because they were women. Their true targets, however, were the working-class, immigrant, and 'racially inferior' mothers who were regarded as the most ignorant of all.

The postwar establishment of a federal health department with special divisions for maternal and child welfare, and the adoption of a similar framework in provincial and municipal governments, facilitated attempts to modernize motherhood. Municipal governments in larger centres added to their pre-war networks of well-baby clinics and expanded their roster of visiting nurses, while many smaller towns, on the urging of provincial health officials, also attempted these services. The effectiveness of the clinic and visiting-nurse networks was directly related to the density of population. Sparsely settled districts on the prairies and in the northern reaches rarely saw such services, except for occasional provincial travelling clinics, or through the sporadic efforts of church missionary organizations, local women's groups, and the Red Cross. In Newfoundland, nursing stations were set up in outports under the auspices of the Grenfell Mission, established in the late nineteenth century by the Social Gospel–inspired medical missionary Wilfred Grenfell.

If state involvement in family life became more apparent in the postwar years, it had been the basis of Aboriginal citizenship since the land treaties and the establishment of the reserve system in the nineteenth century. First Nations people were designated as children of the paternal state, their lives on the reserves always subject to the decisions of the Indian Affairs Department. In all too many communities, the death rate so exceeded the rate of natural increase that it appeared to some observers that 'the race' would soon disappear. Dr Peter Bryce, a leader in the public-health movement and the first federal official directly responsible for Native health, published his investigation of conditions at industrial and residential schools on the prairies in 1922 as *The Story of a National Crime: An Appeal for Justice for the Indians of Canada*. He revealed that, in one decade alone, 25 to 35 per cent of residential-school pupils had died of childhood diseases and tuberculosis. Bryce's requests for school health nurses and tuberculosis prevention and treatment programs were refused. He was successful, however, in implementing visiting-nurse services and in having health- education literature translated into some Aboriginal languages. In 1924, Indian Affairs took official responsibility for the Inuit, extending its limited medical services into the eastern Arctic. Real progress, however, was impeded by the government's commitment to 'education' and 'Canadianization' as the answer to family problems in these communities.

Although prenatal medical supervision was strongly r
mended by MacMurchy and given much rhetorical su
by doctors and public-health officials, many women still experienced pregnancy and childbirth without medical attention. The problem was exacerbated by sparse settlement and
geographic isolation, but it was fairly common in towns and
cities, where many families simply could not pay the high costs
of private physician care. When women's groups lobbied the
provincial and federal governments for licensed midwives,
organized medicine successfully countered their petitions.
Working-class, immigrant, rural, and Aboriginal women
across the country continued to give birth at home, at times
with trained midwives, other times with only neighbours and
kin to assist, only rarely with doctor assistance. In 1920s Saskatchewan, one woman recalled, the nearest doctor was often 'too far to come for a baby,' so her mother would simply
'pitch in and do the job. She delivered whole families, getting up at all times of the night when somebody came and
said she was needed. She never had any nursing training but
she was nurse and doctor too.'

Scientific Childrearing: Training Modern Mothers

If numbers of families reached is any measure, the most successful aspect of the campaign for scientific motherhood was
the mass production of advice literature. In government-
published pamphlets and manuals, approved principles of
modern family life were compressed into directives to rem-
edy maternal ignorance and 'upgrade' family living. The
production of childrearing information was not in itself new
to the 1920s. What was 'modern' about this advice was the
fact that it was predominantly medical in authorship and that
the state took active part in its production and distribution.
Childrearing information was further popularized in the
advice columns and women's sections of mass-circulation
magazines and newspapers, through radio shows, the news-
reels that introduced feature films in this period, travelling

promotional displays, domestic-science classes, 'Little Mothers Clubs' in schools, women's groups and church missionary societies, and insurance and pharmaceutical companies. In Quebec, and in francophone communities elsewhere, parish priests often distributed French-language versions of federal Health Department and Council on Child and Family Welfare publications.

The parenting literature's immediate purpose was to promote improved health and hygienic standards. Far from being purely informative, however, it was also intentionally 'formative.' Much of the state-produced literature was directly influenced by the views of Dr Alan Brown, chief of Toronto's Hospital for Sick Children, and consultant and overseer to municipal, provincial, and federal health departments. Brown's popular manual, *The Normal Child: Its Care and Feeding* (1923), captured the postwar desire to define and promote 'normalcy.' Many Canadians of the time were convinced that there existed an 'ideal child' who represented the best future for modern Canada. Imitating Brown's tone as well as his advice, the literature uniformly strove to establish doctors as maternal mentors and child saviours, to associate maternity with national interest, to reformulate motherhood, and to reconstruct 'the family.' Doctors would be overseers, training and supervising mothers so that they, in turn, could 'manage' their pregnancies effectively and efficiently to produce the ideal modern child. Under continued medical direction, the child was further 'managed' by its mother all along the way to attaining its adult potential as a model citizen. Victorian notions about the fragility and innocence of children and their need for insulation from the corruptions of the adult world gave way to views of children as 'raw material.' Careful parental handling would transform them into 'little machines,' the ultimate evolutionary condition for modern citizens of the Machine Age.

Although they consistently used the language of science, the core concept informing the experts' childrearing prescriptions was management. The application of scientific management – or Taylorism, after its theorist, American engineer Frederick Winslow Taylor – to the home presided over by women would be just as beneficial as it was in the masculine workplace. Idealized modern motherhood was infused with the spirit of industry, with its demands for regularity, repetition, scheduling, systematization, discipline, and productivity. The 'kitchen timepiece is the most important tool of modern childrearing,' proclaimed eminent Canadian child psychologist Dr William Blatz. According to the behaviourist theories of his American colleague John B. Watson, which were very influential during the 1920s, every child could be 'conditioned' to respond to maternal directives – providing that mothers themselves remained emotionally detached, 'in control,' and committed to the program. 'A great deal of letting alone' was advised by all experts. Over-handling and misguided displays of affection meant that 'many a grown-up neurotic can trace his troubles to an unquiet babyhood.' Such 'unemotional' and 'objective' scientific childrearing would not only protect infants from unnecessary exposure to germs, but also guarantee the necessary development of independence and self-control.

We cannot assume that the 'perfect modern mother' roles depicted in the advice literature actually reflected widespread parenting experiences, nor can we assume that they were implemented by the majority of even the keenest would-be modern mothers. Doctors, and other supporters of the ideal modern family, fretted and expounded so much because they recognized that no amount of propaganda, regulation, and surveillance, however unprecedented, was sufficient to stamp out choice or to dictate what ultimately happened in private homes. Judging by the testimony of mothers themselves, they incorporated into their practices those ideas that best suited them in terms of practicality, personality, and economics. Women appreciated the clinics, the literature, and the visiting- nurse services, especially in frontier and resource communities. As a rural mother wrote to the Council on Child and Family Welfare, 'it means a whole lot to have such splendid advice and assistance offered to us free and from such a reliable source.'

Mothers were also critical of the campaign's invasive aspects, however, and not entirely convinced of the benefits of 'expertise' over time-honoured methods and the traditional network of advisers represented by their own mothers, female kin, friends, and neighbours. Those who were isolated because of geography, poverty, and 'foreignness' took what help they could get from Canadians who otherwise ignored or disdained them. But they bridled at the sense of superiority that usually underlay it. As the experience of Ukrainian prairie women reveals, the immigrant group's own elite at times joined in the denigration of Old World childrearing customs, supporting the 'English' model. The unwavering commitment to maternal education at the expense of real medical services, and the continued dismissal of poverty as a health issue, meant that training poor mothers in modern principles of childcare and family living was often futile. In the end, no legislation was enacted during this time to ensure adequate maternal and child health services for needy families, notwithstanding the rhetorical value given to maternity.

Modern Problems: 'Flaming Youth,' Sexuality, and Birth Control

Despite the talk of a 'new morality,' sex education was still widely considered the duty of parents, primarily mothers, and regarded as best left to the home. In Catholic and public school systems alike, teaching was limited mostly to the familiar injunctions against sexual expression outside marriage, including masturbation, and to urging self-control within. The few available publications, in English and in French, explicitly warned readers about the hazards of sex as much as they provided clinical information. The memories of women from Montreal working-class families reveal that many did not even understand the basic physical aspects of sexual relations until their wedding nights. During her first pregnancy, one woman had to ask her neighbour 'how the baby would get out.' Likewise, a Toronto woman was hospitalized for two weeks to await the birth of her first child when her doctor discovered that she 'didn't know which way the baby was coming.' Mothers were advised to tell their daughters 'the facts of life,' but many modern girls remained ill-informed, if not misinformed.

Prevailing constructions of manliness and the persistent double standard turned a blind eye to premarital experimentation by young men, on the other hand. It was expected that boys would learn about sex at some point in early adolescence. For many, wartime experience overseas had included sexual initiation, as they were removed from familial surveillance and presented with opportunities free of the usual restraints. Because of the threats to physical and moral health that soldiers allegedly confronted in Europe, social purity and public-health advocates waged their own war against venereal diseases through educational campaigns. Their concerns about health and 'racial degeneration' were also about the sexual corruption of innocent young men exposed to 'foreign' depravities. Except for these campaigns, which combined moral and medical warnings to scare young people into chaste behaviour, efforts to deliver information about healthy sexuality through the schools were not undertaken systematically during the 1920s.

The 'youth problem' that attracted much attention in these years was grounded in public fears about 'the new morality,' and especially about the way that young people appeared to be flouting sexual conventions – or at least aspiring to. Not surprisingly, defenders of the family responded to these dangerous omens with a reassertion of 'traditional' values. Professional journals, newspapers. and popular magazines railed against 'flaming youth,' their defiant clothing, their hairstyles, their slang-filled language, and especially their alleged rejection of manners and participation in lewd pastimes. With its basis in a youthful, mixed-sex pursuit of commercial amusements, popular culture came in for special attack. Press and pulpit, doctors, educators, and reformers, all supported crusades against immodesty of female dress, and 'indecent Negro music' such as jazz and its related styles of 'close' dancing, the tango in particular. Provincial censor boards were created to stand guard over films, the period's foremost source of popular entertainment, which so often depicted a debauched 'Hollywood' lifestyle that might entice and corrupt innocent Canadian youth. In 1919 Monsignor Bruchési, Archbishop of Montreal, appealed to all Quebec Catholics to join the Ligue des bonnes moeurs (the morality league) to combat 'the evils of the present moment.'

The 'youth problem' was regarded as simply another of the troubling manifestations of the crisis in the family, reflecting back on the vacuum of authority at its core. One of the primary objectives of the period's drive for social order, consequently, was to get young people off the streets, out of the 'gangs,' cinemas, and dance halls, and into high schools, vocational training, and morally uplifting youth clubs. Attempts to 'contain' and institutionalize adolescence were evident in the provincial education acts of the early 1920s, which raised the age of school-leaving to sixteen years everywhere except Quebec, and in variations on the Ontario Apprenticeship Act of 1928, which aimed to revive contractual apprenticeship for young men over the age of sixteen. Because rural out-migration was seen as an integral part of the youth problem/family crisis, attempts were made to build a more positive 'modern' image of the countryside in order to keep the young. In Manitoba, farm youth were given explicit messages about the value of farm life through education and community practices intent on fashioning a future of modern farm families. Agricultural techniques taught in the classroom, competition in school and club fairs, and participation in team demonstrations would transform farm boys into agrarian businessmen. Domestic science and home economics programs became part of the core curriculum of elementary and secondary schools, as well as continuing-education courses offered through the agricultural colleges of Guelph

(Ontario) and Manitoba. A system of *écoles ménageres* (house-keeping schools) performed the same service for Quebec women. Such courses aimed to train efficient farm wives, upgrading both household management and management of the farm as a business, while also keeping good Canadian families on the farm.

The perennially contentious issue of family limitation became another important 'problem' of the day. Birth control, a term attributed to U.S. advocate Margaret Sanger, was stridently attacked as 'race suicide' by such prominent figures as Dr J.J. Heagerty, chief of the new federal Health Department (1919). Heagerty espoused the common medical view that attributed the falling birth rate to 'voluntary restriction by the cowardly offspring of Higher Civilization,' a specious practice now 'spreading continually.' The medical profession and its allies in reform, religious, and state circles refused to consider contraception a viable approach to the crisis in the family. Instead, they saw it as a contributing factor. Doctors upheld their right to control contraceptive knowledge, and supported the anti-abortion and anti-contraception platforms of campaigns that were both avidly pro-natalist and sexually repressive. In 1924, the Canadian Birth Control League was formed by British Columbia socialists who also defined the 'birth control problem' in class terms, albeit from a different perspective. As they saw it, doctors, clergy, and other members of the dominant class, with the sanction of the state, were withholding the instruments that would improve the quality of working-class family life in order to ensure a cheap and abundant labour force. The United Church was exceptional in its support of contraception by married couples. Most denominations feared that sexual promiscuity would be the inevitable outcome if the penalty of pregnancy were removed. The Catholic Church proclaimed that any attempt to thwart procreation, even within marriage, was sinful. It did allow married couples to use the 'Oligo-Knauss,' or rhythm, method, still fairly primitive in its understanding of correct timing, but only after consultation with a priest and his blessing. Given the strength of the opposing forces, no cohesive national birth-control movement could take shape during the 1920s.

Protecting Patriarchy: From the Familial to the Social Realm

If the mother-centredness of family life was emphatically reinforced during the maternalist heyday of the 1920s, fathers were obviously still an essential component of the 'normal' family portrait. Families led by women were defined as a 'social problem' not so much because of their precarious economic standing, but because they did not fit the model. The fatherless family – which the Great War had rendered much more visible – was depicted as pathological, hence the emergence of the sociological category 'broken homes.' Curiously, despite the undeniable sociocultural value ascribed to fathers, and the public chorus about family crisis, experts of the time paid little heed to fathers and rarely counselled them about fathering. As fathers came to be identified almost exclusively with providing, new social constructions about fatherhood deemphasized their traditional roles as disciplinarians or moral 'governors,' while simultaneously enhancing maternal responsibility over all aspects of childrearing.

Possibly the shift away from the traditional paternal role made its most profound impact on immigrant fathers. Their customary authority may have been reduced materially by new world conditions that exposed children to the influences of the host culture, and established assimilationist systems and institutions for that very purpose. The impact on the familial role of immigrant women was not so dramatic, largely because their domestic identity as housekeepers and mothers had changed most in its physical setting. According to social workers, the clash between 'the discipline of the old country and the freedom of the new' often resulted in the breakdown of paternal authority, and the 'undoing' of the child. 'He probably knows more at sixteen than I do at fifty,' charged one Italian immigrant of his young son. 'I ask him where he has been or where he is going and he won't say.' Fathers may have felt helpless to 'protect' their children in an environment that they also experienced as new and possibly threatening.

Men's predominant economic roles continued to support male authority in most homes, but prevailing ideas about gender and family supported paternal authority even in situations where women were primary breadwinners. In Paris, Ontario, a textile town with a predominantly female labour force and few job opportunities for men, domestic work was divided pragmatically, according to work schedules. But certain conventional boundaries were maintained. Paris men did not care for children or do laundry, nor, generally, did other unemployed men, or those who worked shifts or on railways or ships where they regularly cooked, cleaned, and served for themselves and others. Inuit men, who took pride in their domestic skills and trained their sons to fend for themselves on hunting trips, also regarded the performance of these tasks in the home as an inappropriate overstepping of their own sphere and interference in women's sphere.

The new domestic expectations of the 1920s confirmed the housewife's role in maintaining an attractive, clean, and harmonious home so that her husband could enjoy his status as 'king of his own castle.' Popular advice literature continually urged women to extend their mothering skills to the care and nurture of husbands. Men carried 'the big responsibilities of life' and needed to replenish themselves in their peaceful homes amidst their loving families after a hard day's labour. By rigidly defining the good wife/mother, they made all the clearer what constituted the husband/father role. In the ideal modern family, fathers were ascribed very narrow role definitions that they themselves may well have found too limited and limiting. They remained the socially sanctioned heads of household and family, however, and were therefore not expected to comply with any infringement of their authority. Moreover, breadwinning was more than financial support, important as that was. It had moral and emotional connotations in relation to wives and children that made men, as providers, worthy of the patriarchal title. While mothers were brought to the fore in the ideal modern family, and fathers were correspondingly relegated to accessory roles, a definite relocation of authority was taking place. The new authorities were not mothers, but 'experts' outside the family circle, often working under the auspices of state agencies.

The most important outcome of the war's effect on families – the absent, dead, or disabled father – along with the determined lobbying of women's groups, paved the way for mothers' allowances. Beginning with Manitoba in 1916, by 1920 mothers' allowances were established in Alberta, Saskatchewan, Ontario, and British Columbia. The very real need of widows for material assistance was acknowledged, but the new welfare legislation was also intended to regulate motherhood. Women's rights to state assistance derived from their reproductive role and their economic dependence on men. Mothers' allowances were needs-based: only mothers with more than one child, who had lost the financial support of their husbands, were entitled to state assistance, and then only if they were widowed or had husbands otherwise incapacitated and unable to provide. Social workers, state agents, and women's organizations alike were leery about assisting deserted, divorced, or unwed mothers, fearing that the status of these women was evidence of their unworthiness. Even 'deserving' widowed mothers had to prove themselves 'fit and proper' persons to raise their own children.

Local gossip and neighbourly surveillance monitored the activities of recipient mothers, particularly with respect to their relationships with men. School attendance, and the behaviour, language, and appearance of children were also measures of maternal fitness, and hence qualification for continued assistance. Families from ethnic minority backgrounds routinely endured even more intense investigation and 'reporting' by neighbours. 'Success stories' often depended on a general 'cleaning up,' as recorded by one investigator, whose initial visit had found a home 'dirty beyond description,' children and mother alike using language that was 'frightful.' After instruction, mother, home, and children were 'the acme of neatness' in what amounted to 'one of the most remarkable cases of social regeneration' the visitor had ever witnessed. Where the family environment remained inadequate, despite regular visitation, advice, and warnings from mothers' allowance workers, the Children's Aid Society removed the children. In 1920, its first year of operation, the Ontario Mothers' Allowance Commission dispensed aid to 2,660 women. By the end of the decade it was helping 5,600 women with almost 17,000 children. The growing number of applications, regardless of the stringent regulations and intrusive procedures, indicates the real need of female-headed families in these years.

There are many other examples of what the state was now prepared to do to bolster the modern family. The first federal income tax, instituted as a war measure in 1917, gave married persons twice the personal exemption given to the unmarried, as a sort of bonus to encourage family formation. Soldiers' allowances and veterans' pensions were determined in part by family status and the number of dependants. Pensions for war widows continued for one year after remarriage, a state dowry recognizing both their first husbands' sacrifice and their own efforts to reconstitute their families. Some provinces adopted parents' maintenance acts to make adult sons and daughters provide financial support for dependent ageing parents, an obligatory family contribution that often took precedence over the means-tested, state-supported old-age pensions of the time. The apparently dramatic increase in desertion immediately following the war also led to tighter laws obliging fathers to maintain their deserted wives and children, and the use of the courts to track them down. In 1917, New Brunswick became the first of a number of English-speaking provinces to follow Quebec's long-standing practice of legitimizing births when the parents subsequently

married each other. Various provincial adoption acts changed
the process from one of indenture – in effect, an economic
relationship with legally specified rights as well as reciprocal
obligations – into a true familial relationship that made
adopted children full members of their receiving families.
The new emphasis on the family as the only appropriate
nurturing environment saw child-welfare workers promote
adoption and fostering over institutional care for neglected,
abandoned, and delinquent children. In 1925, the director
of Toronto's Children's Aid Society reported that the city's
three institutions, once crowded to capacity, altogether
counted only enough resident children to fill one of them.

Following U.S. precedent, reformers also successfully lobbied for the establishment of special family courts in most
provinces, thereby decriminalizing family matters and placing them firmly in the hands of social-work experts. The new
domestic-relations courts emphasized the rehabilition of
families whose home life contrasted negatively with the middle-class ideal. They divided their efforts between keeping an
eye on the morality of mothers, and collecting support money
from fathers, all in the interests of making parents become
appropriate role models. But their primary concern, and
greatest challenge, was keeping parents together for the
children's sake, or getting them to reconcile and at least
appear to be a 'normal' family.

As the family home came to be an indicator of family values, there was much hope that the state could shore up the
family through housing reform, which would help to establish 'ideal surroundings' for a regenerated domesticity. Comfortable and attractive housing came to be seen as essential
to the welfare of working-class families, to their harmonious
relations and their sense of family togetherness. Housing
reformers argued that better housing would relieve the
pressure to escape crowded homes to pursue individualized
leisure activities in disreputable places. Family members,
especially younger ones, would proudly bring in their friends
for healthy recreation, rather than loitering in the streets, tav-

erns, and public spaces where trouble awaited. Arguments for upgraded housing reinforced home and family as key components of respectability, thus appealing strongly to a working class committed to that concept of personal and familial status.

The decentralization of employment and the extension of public transportation during these years encouraged attempts to house the working class away from decaying urban cores, a spatial process that reinforced the separation of work and home begun in the nineteenth century. Suburban projects for ideal family living were inspired by the work of British housing reformers, especially Thomas Adams, whose 'Garden Suburb' designs integrated small parks and public gardens with affordable housing. Adams became the town-planning expert on the Canadian Commission of Conservation in 1914. Motivated by these developments, and jointly funded by private and municipal investment, the Toronto Housing Company built the 'Riverdale Courts' development, east of the Don River, in that year. Its 204 units, called 'cottage flats,' or 'modern apartments,' were arranged in 2 1/2-storey blocks around three landscaped courts. Adams also supervised the reconstruction of Halifax after the 1917 harbour explosion. Instead of the typical working-class single-family dwelling of 'two up, two down,' the new Richmond Hills houses had small parlours, dining rooms and kitchens on the first floor, and three bedrooms on the second floor to permit separate sleeping quarters for parents and for children of each sex. All had electricity, modern bathrooms, kitchen sinks, basement laundries, bedroom closets, and water heaters. Although they attracted tenants and buyers with moderately low incomes, many of these model developments were still beyond the reach of the working poor, for whom the dream home remained only a dream.

Conclusion

While desertion, neglect, abuse, crime, and poverty obviously remained very real domestic issues, there were ways in which families appeared better off in 1930 than they had been in 1914. Improved economic conditions after 1924 made it possible for a small minority of skilled workers' families to attain the 'male breadwinner' domestic ideal. Public-health measures, including vaccination, milk inspection, and extended sanitary regulations, made the heartache and family disruption caused by the early death of a child or a spouse a less common occurrence. Through mothers' allowances and Children's Aid Societies, widows and orphans, and otherwise deserted and neglected women and children, were better provided for by the state than they had ever been. The companionate marriage ideal was certainly an improvement over old models based on patriarchal authority, even while it placed more pressure on young couples to marry carefully, to sustain their marital relationship on a romantic and sexually fulfilling level, and to raise children 'by the book,' all in accordance with the latest expert advice. If contraception were still illegal, couples were choosing to have fewer children. Children lived longer in the family home and also stayed in school longer, thanks in part to rising age limits in compulsory-education legislation and the decline of apprenticeship and child labour. The prevailing ideal at least portrayed family relations as more democratic, companionable, and affectionate. Increasingly, measures were being taken by outside agencies towards achieving that end through public education and active intervention where deemed necessary.

'The family' and all its problems, real and imagined, became more the subject of public discussion during the tumultuous years between the Great War and the Great Depression than it had ever previously been. As the 'traditional family' adapted to modernization, the idealized middle-class family – breadwinner father, dependent household-manager/wife, and carefully trained dependent children – became an ever-stronger public image. These developments included the increasing subjection of modern families to the scrutiny of new family experts and agencies, although intervention was restricted to a minority of 'problem' families. The new model modern family, much like 'the family' of tradition, contradicted lived experience for many Canadians. Never was this contrast between ideal and reality more apparent than during the Great Depression of the 1930s.

PART III
FACING THE WALL:
ENDURING THE GREAT DEPRESSION

5

Families in Distress: Surviving the 'Dirty Thirties'

The Depression lore of Canada is replete with family trag-
edies. In 1934, a Winnipeg woman on relief drowned her
eighteen-month-old son, strangled her five-year-old daughter, and poisoned herself with germicide bought on credit
from a drugstore. A Ukrainian immigrant was sentenced to
three months in prison for killing a moose and her calf to
feed his family of six. Refusing the sterilization that was also
part of his penalty, he was deported with his family. When
his small business failed like so many others, a lumberyard
manager in Camrose, Alberta, shot and killed his wife and
two daughters, then drowned himself. A despondent farmer
in Ste-Perpetue, Quebec, battered his four sleeping children
with a hammer. The often-recounted story of the Bates family of Saskatchewan is particularly nightmarish. Despairing
after repeated attempts to 'start over,' their planned family
suicide by carbon monoxide in their car took only the life of
their beloved young son. The jury that heard their case refused to convict them of murder. The boy's killer, the jurists
declared, was the Depression itself, specifically the ineffec-
tual government policies which had driven so many Canadians to the edge, and some beyond. Such instances, thankfully,
do not represent the common experience of Depression-
era families in Canada, although we can only guess at the
extent of domestic strife caused by material want and

insecurity. But to those intently charting its progress, the 'crisis in the family' appeared to be reaching its apex during the 1930s.

This chapter considers how Canadian families coped with the destabilizing impact of the Depression, particularly its differential age and gender consequences. It also discusses evolving theories and policies regarding families, as family experts and governments tried to come to terms with the crisis at hand. Whatever the difficulties of generalization about family experiences, the 1930s posed a clear challenge to the social order. The Great Depression stripped the mystifying veils from a system ordered by fundamental inequalities, and a state lacking both the ideological commitment and the structural mechanisms to meet the social troubles that ensued.

Like the Industrial Revolution and the Great War, the Depression constituted a moment of 'punctuated equilibrium.' It brought into bold relief the underlying contradictions, emerging challenges, and material and ideological changes affecting Canadian families. In the atmosphere of urgency caused by the mounting unemployment of male breadwinners, families were impelled to respond and restabilize, often turning back to such traditional resources as home production, assistance from kin, and participation in an 'informal' economy that customarily involved the labour of women and children. If the Great War ushered in the era of the 'modern family,' the Great Depression demonstrated just how fragile were some of its material foundations.

The Bottom Falls Out: Material Effects

The downturn in the U.S. economy sparked by the collapse of the New York Stock Exchange in October 1929 was quickly felt in Canada. But the Depression was more than simply an effect of the Crash: it was the first great crisis of modern capitalism, international in nature and scope. With 80 per cent of its farm, forest, and mine production sold abroad, the

Canadian resource economy was vulnerable and ill-protected against any decline in foreign demand. The available statistics probably obscure the true extent of national unemployment. They do reveal that more Canadians were out of work during the 1930s than ever before or since, and for longer periods. By March 1931, the number of jobless passed 400,000, representing almost 20 per cent of the non-agricultural labour force. At the darkest point, during the winter of 1933, estimates prepared for Conservative prime minister R.B. Bennett revealed that 32.1 per cent of wage earners were unemployed. After a decade of increasing material expectations and consumer expenditures, personal savings were negative from 1931 through 1933, as Canadians used up whatever they had to tide them over. For those whose standard of living was already at subsistence level or close to it, there was nothing to cushion the fall into destitution. In Montreal, the centre of Quebec's industrial activity, 87 per cent of heads of working-class families were on relief. In the West, falling wheat prices, prolonged drought, soil drifting, and plagues of grasshoppers devastated the prairie economy and the farm families at its base. Never having enjoyed an equitable share in industrial growth, the Maritime provinces saw an accelerating decline in exports and per-capita income. Devastated by the collapse of its resource economy, Newfoundland, which would not enter Confederation until 1949, surrendered its sovereignty to a British-appointed commission of government in 1934. British Columbia became a 'fair weather' mecca for the single unemployed, a situation that sparked fear among its residents and public cries for defensive barriers against the westward march of the dispossessed.

Much of the distress of the 1930s resulted from inadequate and ill-organized relief efforts. The expectation was simply that the municipalities, assisted by private charities, would continue their historic role of providing relief for the deserving poor. The Bennett Relief Act of 1930 allotted $16 million for public works, divided among the provinces on the basis of population rather than need. The provinces gave to municipalities what remained of these funds after meeting their own budgetary requirements. Cash-strapped municipalities did not have the necessary infrastructure to coordinate an effective system so that relief could be distributed fairly on the only basis that counted, that of need. The built-in expedients, therefore, were those of convention and common prejudice. Married men got preference over the unmarried of both sexes. British subjects were preferred over immigrants. Women, Aboriginals, Asians, and any people of colour were at the bottom of every list. Increasingly rigid residence qualifications were enforced, as more families, but especially young single men, became transient in hopes of bettering their luck 'somewhere else.'

Those who ultimately qualified for relief work found themselves confronting more administrative arbitrariness. The same allotment of work was given to each male applicant regardless of the size of his family or the duration of his joblessness. There were great discrepancies in relief allotments between provinces, even between neighbouring municipalities. A London, Ontario, family of five, for example, received $40.39 per month for food, fuel, and shelter – already inadequate – but that same family received only $18.86 in Halifax. In Toronto, allowances were 40 per cent below the minimum standards for health acknowledged by the medical profession. Incredibly, relief payments in Nova Scotia's industrial towns of Sydney, Glace Bay, New Waterford, and Springhill averaged about $4 per month. New Brunswick and Prince Edward Island cut off most relief payments in the summer, forcing many of their municipalities to do likewise. Across Canada, those still working often found their earnings so deflated that a large proportion received little more than relief wages for their labour.Clothing workers in Montreal and Toronto, many of them women who were now the family breadwinners, earned only $10.00 for a sixty-hour week.

The distribution of relief was the work of an ill-coordinated collection of private charities and emergency relief committees, again at the municipal level where the new experts in social welfare and social work had as yet little influence. The 'dole,' as the allowance came to be known, was given to applicants once they had proved their destitution by exhausting every personal and familial resource. In some municipalities, all 'unnecessary' possessions – such luxuries as cars, radios, telephones, and liquor permits – had to be relinquished. Relief was depicted as charity, and charity was limited to those evidently deserving the pity of strangers. The process required a certain abasement on the part of applicants to ensure their honesty, their humble appreciation, and a measure of shame that would keep them mindful of their responsibility to avoid the 'pauperism' of dependence on the state. Because the most 'deserving' applicants were male heads of families, this responsibility centred on the material support of wives and children. After waiting in line for hours, in church basements, firehalls, and other public buildings, applicants had to answer a list of personal questions and swear to their own destitution, a public admission of their inability to provide. 'I've seen tears in a man's eyes,' reported one relief administrator, 'as though they were signing away their manhood and their right to be a husband and sit at the head of a table.' In the context of contemporary ideals about gender and family, they were. These men could no longer perform the functions that secured their status. Disempowered by their inability to provide and protect, they became something less than true men.

To ward off the spectre of mass pauperization that so haunted middle-class Canadians, the provision of cash to 'reliefers' was initially avoided. Food vouchers to be redeemed at local stores effectively placed them under the watch of their neighbours, discouraging the 'undeserving' and those inclined to spend on 'wrong' purchases. Clothing was second-hand, adding to the humiliation of families receiving the discards of their more fortunate neighbours. One woman remembered the mortification she felt when, as a ten-year-old, she found herself sitting in church near the original owner of her coat. In the early years, most municipalities also refused to pay rent, placing families at the mercy of already-strapped landlords. Reliefers were often required to cut their own wood for fuel, and perform other types of manual labour. This was meant both as repayment for the assistance they received, and to forestall the loss of their initiative to provide. As it was in the Victorian era, the propensity to work was regarded as a fragile instinct needing vigilant protection. In addition to their unresponsive governments, Canadians also blamed immigrants for their suffering. The so-called bohunk invasion became a popular theme for aspiring demagogues, despite the fact that immigration was virtually halted by restrictive legislation in 1930. The large number of single men who had arrived just before the Crash were more transient than most workers, since they had few local and familial roots and performed as a dispensable reserve army of unskilled labour. They were a highly visible contingent of the single unemployed 'on the tramp' through the West in those years, often the targets of an anti-communism never far from the surface of postwar racism and xenophobia. Their plans for a profitable sojourn in ashes, many of these men were unable to repay money borrowed for fares, to bring out their families, or to return home on their own account. The state's stand on unemployed immigrants and their families was harsh and uncompromising. Between 1930 and 1935, 28,000 men, women, and children were deported because of their alleged radicalism – defined primarily by union membership – because they had somehow come up against the law, or simply because they had applied for relief. Many had Canadian-born children. In some cases, entire families were deported even when the wife was self-supporting or living apart from her husband.

Aboriginals and Canadian-born people of colour fared no better than did 'foreigners.' In the Maritimes, where many Native and African-Canadians eked out a living by combining agriculture or handicraft production with wage labour, their modest family economies were reduced to serious hardship. Native people's relationship with the federal government actually encouraged overt discrimination against them. Employers and relief committees rationalized that, as wards of the state, they needed neither jobs nor regular assistance. In Nova Scotia, municipal officials protested against including African-Canadians in provincial medical-relief plans, resisting the application of local taxes in this manner. In 1937, a mob of 400 destroyed the home of a Black family that had bought a house in a white neighbourhood in Trenton.

Relief administrators, struggling with immense caseloads and obliged to stretch scarce funds, were frustrated and demoralized by the inadequate provisions made for those in need. The bare-bones relief regulations allowed nothing for medical care, soap, toiletries. Milk was severely restricted, often permitted only to infants and invalids. As a result, a Sydney, Nova Scotia, family of ten, with a tubercular mother, could have only a single pint of milk each day. If more than one dollar was earned by any family member, that sum was extracted from the already-miserly food allowance. Growing up in a small Ontario town, one man recalled that he did not taste fruit until the age of eighteen, when he enlisted for service in the Second World War. Nor was recreation for those forced into abundant leisure considered an appropriate concern of the state. There was no allotment for any kind of reading material, including newspapers, and certainly none for the ten-cent movies that were the pastime of the age, much less the debaucheries represented by alcohol and cigarettes. All these were denied the destitute, whose moral core was already worn, as their destitution itself signified. Relief was a character judgment. Survival was all that the state and society owed to these failed providers and their families. Even the strict criteria and deliberate stigma could not mask the extent of real need, however. In April 1935, those dependent on relief numbered 1.9 million, or nearly 20 per cent of the Canadian population. Because relief fell largely on the municipal governments whose coffers were eroded as tax revenues declined and expenditures skyrocketed, many municipalities were on the verge of fiscal collapse, or already there, by mid-decade. Things appeared both hopeless and desperate.

The Quality of Life: Health and Family Welfare

The length and severity of the Depression provided irrefutable evidence of the relationship between poverty and health. Widely acknowledged as the most sensitive index of living standards, the infant mortality rate rose from 70.8 to 73.6 per 1,000 live births between 1932 and 1933, an increase of 421 baby deaths from one year to the next. The Council on Child and Family Welfare's national study of maternal mortality, released in 1935, acknowledged that a significant percentage of maternal and neonatal deaths was due to the mothers' 'impaired health generally,' and warned that the impact of childhood malnourishment would continue to show in future generations. This heavy increase in infant mortality was partially responsible for upward movement in the general mortality rate. Averaging 9.7 per 100,000 from 1931 to 1935, the index rose to 10.2 in 1937.

Many of the health problems of Canadian families were due to lack of proper nourishment and medical care. In drought-stricken southern Saskatchewan, people lived on rabbits and boiled Russian thistle. In Toronto, author Charles Templeton remembers that he, his mother, and three siblings could not stretch their weekly food allotment past the sixth day, and often had only water to relieve hunger on the seventh. A diet of potatoes and lard was all-too-common for many Canadians, as documented in the countless plaintive letters begging aid from millionaire Prime Minister R.B. Bennett. The Toronto Committee for Dietary Studies, in a two-year food consumption survey of 100 lower-income families published in 1940, found that only 3 of these families could secure the caloric supply recommended as the Canadian dietary standard.

And so growing numbers of ill-nourished children contracted deficiency diseases such as rickets and pellagra, and were predisposed to any disease that came along and attacked bodies with little resistance. Medical school inspections in Montreal diagnosed a wide variety of diseases affecting at least 50 per cent of all children examined through the decade, few of whom received the medical attention advised. Among the nation's Aboriginal families, persistent high infant mortality, general ill health, and lowered life expectancy testified to the continued poverty and scarcity of medical care. By the 1930s, the Medical Branch of the Department of Indian Affairs was responsible for the health services of 112,500 people spread over 800 communities.

It was only under the auspices of medical relief services established in some provinces by mid-decade that many Canadians attained access to care priced out of their means even during prosperous times. Like all other types, it was grudging relief. In one area of Winnipeg, 16,000 patients were served by one relief doctor, and there was no dentist. Continued concern about mothers and infants saw some special services developed for them, at the same time that many of the established free clinics and nurse visits were curtailed or abandoned. Under Toronto's Maternal Welfare Service for indigent mothers, instigated in September 1933, the city accepted financial responsibility for the home confinement of indigent patients, or for their hospitalization if necessary, after determining both the home's suitability and the family's financial eligibility. In Montreal, the Assistance maternelle also confirmed the indigence of beneficiaries before sending home visitors and providing free medical assistance to needy prospective mothers. Cottage hospitals funded by the Women's Missionary Society of the United Church served isolated districts in the North and on the prairies, as did the Red Cross Hospital-on-Wheels. In Newfoundland, a cottage hospital scheme, with eighteen small hospitals strategically located in larger towns, attempted to supplement the work of the traditional outport 'granny-midwives.' The philanthropic Grenfell Association also set up a half-dozen cottage hospitals in Labrador, primarily to attend to the needs of the

Inuit population. For the most part, however, rural and out-post mothers across the nation still depended almost exclusively on the services of neighbours and untrained local midwives. Impoverished expectant mothers wrote to the prime minister, the federal Health Department, and the council about their inability to pay the $15 to $25 fee that most doctors asked for attendance at confinements. Not even evidence of the great need, and continued high maternal and infant mortality rates, could persuade doctors to share the care of parturient women with trained and licensed midwives. Yet 98 per cent of Canadian women still gave birth at home; in 1936, 13.2 per cent of these births were without physician attendance.

Upsetting the Natural Order: The Crisis of Unemployed Breadwinners

The coping strategies of Depression-era families were clearly pragmatic reactions to immediate material pressures, but they also reflected ongoing trends. As we have seen, the 'culture of abundance' arising from the pumped-up consumer economy of the 1920s made itself felt primarily in middle-class families. But the desires created and promoted through popular culture raised expectations for all Canadians, in whatever measure they could actually afford the new products or imitate a middle-class lifestyle. Economic hardship was certainly nothing new for some Canadian families, who had endured it even during the so-called Roaring Twenties. What was new in the 'Dirty Thirties' was the extent of deprivation, and, even more important, the fact that the trauma associated with unemployment and loss of property affected families previously enjoying some protection against them. The work of a lifetime, symbolized by savings, a house, a farm, new products for the home, a car, or even just hopes and plans for a better future, evaporated when families were suddenly unable to pay their bills.

The Depression created two distinct classes of the poor that eclipsed the conventional moralist dichotomies of deserving/ undeserving and respectable/unrespectable. The traditional poor, whose economic marginality was already established before the 1930s, and whose numbers had been slowly rising even in prosperity, included woman-headed families, the disabled, the elderly, Aboriginals, people of colour, recently arrived immigrants, and many families of unskilled labourers. The new poor were the hundreds of thousands of formerly self-sustaining middle-class and working-class families now thrown into penury. The families of the traditional poor were accustomed to functioning as economic units. The newly poor found that their survival now depended on an internal restructuring of roles and relations in the absence of adequate external assistance. In many ways, the Depression necessitated a return to the family model that middle-class, and more prosperous working-class families, had been slowly moving away from: that of the interdependent family economy. Anything that any family member could contribute by way of wages or production took on new importance. While this usually entailed additional labour and responsibility for women, it did not strike at the very heart of feminine identities in the way that the loss of provider status affected men.

With the onslaught of the Depression, many women who had never before worked for wages were obliged to seek work. The crisis initially spurred female labour-force participation. As men lost jobs in manufacturing and in the primary sectors, lesser-paid wives and daughters picked up jobs in the service and finance sectors that were not hit as fast. The federal government's Special Committee on Price Spreads (1934) found that, with very few exceptions, women were working for wages because of necessity, not personal choice. Despite the circumstances, the paid employment of women was interpreted more vehemently than ever as a threat to the rightful position of men, to the family, and to capitalist society. Organized labour, the National Council of Women, and even some business and professional women's clubs, officially

deplored the employment of married women. They proposed, instead, the historic solution to the problem of wom-
en's labour: domestic service, the most gender-typed of all
wage work. The question of working women was fundamental to the social-policy debates of those years and how these
were ultimately encoded in legislation. Gender and marital
status determined not only the experience of unemployed
workers throughout the Depression, but also the nature of
welfare policy long after its end.

Although the unemployment of husbands did not always
result in the employment of wives, disruptions of the taken-
for-granted triad of male provider/husband/father roles
could not help but affect relationships as well as material
security. The crisis of unemployed breadwinners also intensified the complementary and 'natural' role of women as
nurturing, supportive wives and mothers. Whether or not
they took on paid labour, wives and children were often
burdened with the social and psychological repercussions of
male unemployment. Few adult men had spent much time
in the home, and few had practical knowledge of its day-to-
day routines. Among Montreal working-class families, even
men accustomed to periodic unemployment had difficulty
coming to terms with the loss of provider status that made
them self-defined 'pauvres honteux,' an expression that cap-
tures their shame at finding themselves in a condition to be
pitied. One man 'cried like an infant' when the philanthropic
St Vincent de Paul Society conducted its requisite 'house
check' before permitting his family direct relief; he recalled
a desperate self-loathing inspired by the knowledge that he
had 'two good arms, two good legs,' yet was unable to support his own family. His self-characterization suggests that,
quite literally, only someone who was less than a man would
come to such a state. Many Canadian women, looking back
over their Depression experiences, clearly remembered their
husbands' humiliation at having to report weekly to the same
municipal bureaucrats, to line up with shamefaced patience
for the vouchers that kept their families alive.

Women were frequently constrained to be supportive and tolerant, not only because of their social conditioning and customary family roles, but also because their individual prospects were darker than ever. If the Depression delayed marriages, it likely prolonged a great many for the simple purpose of survival. One Saskatchewan woman found her husband's rages about crop failures and bad times 'sapping her health,' but held on because of their young daughter, whom it would 'hurt dreadfully to say anything against her dad.' The modern family, based on a companionate ideal that intimated a partnership of equals, might try to suppress its traditional patriarchal core, but could not deny it – especially not in times of stress, as some working-class families had probably long known. Once the 'natural' order of things was upset, subordination to the husband/father might continue through habit and even will. But, given the integral role of provider to masculine identities and family relations, loss of that role might disturb the concept of the husband/father's prerogatives, straining relationships all round. One of the most serious effects of the Depression for middle-class families was the way that it shattered their belief in the possibility of a security that depended entirely on the male breadwinner.

In general, where domestic roles were clearly defined and accepted, and where family relations were founded on mutual respect and complementarity, the Depression does not seem to have had devastating effects on family unity. The male-breadwinner ideal gave considerable weight to conventional gender and family constructions despite the circumstances that made them clearly impracticable. Whether or not they went out to work, most women maintained their traditional roles even as men lost theirs. There remained at least a façade of the traditional family to present to the outside world and to organize relations within. In families where this ideal had always been elusive, the Depression likely did not bring about much change in roles and relations. More African-Canadian women now became the sole support of families, for example, but working for wages was nothing new to these women, always disproportionately represented among working married women.

Making Do and Getting By: Family Strategies

For most stricken families, the first, and perhaps the only possible, strategy was acceptance of a lower standard of living, the absence of choice belying the concept of 'strategy.' The Depression tended to blur class boundaries, as joblessness affected all occupational categories. Even in families where the father held on to a job, wage cuts or shortened hours were common, and job insecurity was endemic, compelling strict economies. All families ultimately relied more heavily on women's traditional capacity to 'make do' and stretch household dollars. Reversing pre-Depression consumer trends, only the minimum purchases were made, and women produced the maximum in terms of goods and services. Mending, sewing, backyard vegetable gardens, berry-picking, baking, and canning returned to many homes, and the recycling of clothes and other goods enjoyed a vogue largely forgotten since the shortages caused by war. Carefully bleached to remove the brand names, cotton flour and sugar bags were turned into sheets, towels, and even shirts and dresses. The milder climate of British Columbia allowed children to go barefoot through late spring and summer, sparing their families the expense of shoes. When clothes and shoes were past patching and no donations were forthcoming, people just stayed home. As author James Gray remembered those 'winter years,' the close confinement of women to the home, 'with a couple of children under foot' and 'without the simple diversions and excursions that a good dress could provide,' were especially trying. Yet previous experiences of unemployment and constrained family budgets prepared many working-class families to meet Depression scarcity with well-honed resourcefulness. The conditions of unemployment were not so much a drastic change as another dimension of working-class life, made worse by the current crisis, but still familiar.

Participation in the informal or 'hidden' economy continued to be an important means of balancing family needs and scarce income, especially in situations where domestic responsibilities made it difficult for women to join the labour force even if there were jobs available. Because any income at all was counted against relief received – and because relief alone barely kept body and soul together – many women, men, and children were likely supplementing their meagre resources with 'moonlighting.' Some of it, like making and selling bootleg whisky and running gaming houses, was illegal. Author Denise Chong's immigrant grandmother ran Mah-Jong games from her lodgings in Vancouver's Chinatown in addition to waiting on tables. A Montreal widow opened a small restaurant in her home, let rooms, and took in sewing; still unable to support her children on her own, she felt her only recourse was to remarry. Aboriginal women in British Columbia returned to such traditional subsistence pursuits as gathering plant foods and collecting shellfish. Most of these women were doing much as working-class women had always done by using all possible resources, and their own labour, to bolster the family economy. The difference was that their contributions, usually supplementary, now became the only family income.

Doubling-up and overcrowding in accommodation were strategies of despair for many families, as moves to ever cheaper, smaller, and unhealthier lodgings became an everyday parade. Housing surveys undertaken in Montreal, Ottawa, Toronto, and Winnipeg discovered a serious shortage of habitable low-rent dwellings. As corporations cut expenditures, those in company towns saw bad conditions deteriorate further. Although there was coal everywhere in the mining town of Glace Bay, Nova Scotia, the company police kept close guard over the supply. Driftwood, picket fences, shingles, clapboard, even telephone poles were burned to keep people from freezing to death. The Souris coalfields of southern Saskatchewan had families housed in tarpaper shacks amidst the heaps of slag. One family of eleven, living in a one-bedroom plywood shack, often woke to a snow-covered floor on winter mornings. The problem of decent, affordable accommodation was not new, but it was now affecting much larger numbers, and was no longer limited to the lower stratum of the working class. After many years of refusing all municipal and provincial pleas for assistance, the federal government came up with the Dominion Housing Act of 1935, which became the National Housing Act in 1938. The acts were intended to provide low-cost home-building loans to encourage those with steady incomes to invest their money in new houses. Like previous attempts to facilitate low-cost housing, however, they did little for the families most in need.

The Depression also tended to reverse earlier steps towards a universally protected childhood. The children of the unemployed and the working poor were the prime casualties of the economic crisis, but middle-class children also had to be socialized to adapt to pressing economic realities. In many homes, children again took on adult responsibilities at an early age. Pooling family incomes provided a necessary buffer against loss of work. Part-time jobs for children – running errands, mowing lawns, babysitting, selling newspapers and magazines, shining shoes, carting groceries, or returning pop bottles for pennies – were strategies familiar to working-class families, and now more significant to middle-class family economies than in more prosperous times. For some, lack of adequate food and clothing impeded regular school attendance. Some urban school boards provided hot lunches, free milk, and clothing for needy children, relying largely on private charity. Barely able to pay their teachers' salaries, they were forced to turn a blind eye to irregular attendance.

The help of kin and family still went a long way. Support from kin kept some families off the relief rolls, and helped to 'tide over' families where underemployment and wage cuts caused difficulties. Young married couples and their children moved in with parents where the older breadwinner had kept his job, or elderly parents moved in with children. Young people, especially young women, were more or less forced to stay home and depend on their families, or give whatever they could earn to the family's upkeep. At the age of twenty-six, one Maritime seafarer supported his brother, mother, and father on his wages of $65 per month in the lighthouse service, the only money entering the home. All he kept for himself was enough to buy a weekly package of tobacco. At times, country relatives, otherwise penniless but at least able to feed their families from their own production, sent fresh produce and milk to their unemployed urban kin. A jobless Sydney, Nova Scotia, steelworker attributed the survival of his family – on relief totalling a dollar per week per person – to the assistance of his farmer brother-in-law, who brought weekly donations of milk.

Working-class family members also tended to live close to one another in cities, however much they moved around within their neighbourhoods. This proximity facilitated exchange of clothing, shoes, and services, including the borrowing and lending of tools and equipment, or the use of washing machines and telephones. Sisters might exchange chores, one doing the washing for two families while the other did the ironing; mothers and mothers-in-law minded children while daughters did their heavier cleaning and laundry for them. Having left the reserves for industrial employment in the years since the First World War, many Six Nations families in Ontario returned during the 1930s, so that they could at least grow their own food and share housing with other family members. These earlier, traditional patterns of family mutuality and reciprocity were especially valuable resources during the 1930s. But even the cross-generational resources of many working-class families could not stretch very far, making relief or 'riding the rails' a likely prospect for younger male members.

To some observers, the Depression appeared an important lesson in family solidarity. In contrast to the 1920s trend towards increasing separation of home and leisure, especially for youth, the lack of money for commercialized recreation meant that more people looked to the family circle for fun. Visiting with family and friends continued to be important, although many reported that it fell off as hosts became ashamed of their inability to offer refreshments, and guests reluctant to take advantage of the limited resources of others. Card-playing and other 'parlour games' remained popular. Librarians noted that reading had increased tremendously since the beginning of the Depression, and community gardening was also touted as both moral and physical nourishment for the unemployed and their families. Among the 'modern' leisure pursuits, author James Gray recalled that 'radio-listening was a passion that the unemployed shared with the employed, the rich shared with the poor.' The radio allowed prairie families to escape Depression suffering, the dust, and the merciless wind 'that blew night and day with its incessant, deranging whine.' Radio also added to the popularity of spectator sports, especially hockey: in Toronto in 1931, despite Depression constraints, $1.6 million was raised in six months to build Maple Leaf Gardens, Canada's spectacular modern arena, home of the revered Toronto Maple Leafs hockey team. The movies remained a relatively cheap source of amusement for the Depression-weary. In 1930, there were 910 theatres in Canada. In 1934, for Canada as a whole, attendance reached a total of 107,718,000 people, with Ontario accounting for almost half that number, and Quebec about one-quarter. Hollywood capitalized on the public's need for escapism with gangster films, grand-scale musicals, and fluffy romantic comedies, the last named often featuring such famous child stars as Shirley Temple and Mickey Rooney.

Fewer Mouths to Feed: The Birth-Control Movement

Family limitation was another of the continuities of family life and marital relations that took on new significance because of the economic crisis, becoming a necessarily more common family strategy. Delayed marriage was the first step for many couples: only 62,000 marriages were formalized in 1932, a decline of 12 per cent since the 1920s, and a twentieth-century low of 6.5 marriages per 1,000 people. For the first time since official records were kept in 1851, the number of births actually dropped between two decennial censuses, from 2.42 million during the 1920s to 2.29 million for the 1930s. By 1941, the average number of children per family had declined to 2.7. The decline is explained in part by delayed marriages, but it was also due to deliberate family limitation by couples who simply could not feed any more mouths and could not envision better times.

The Depression emergency catalysed the birth-control movement in Canada. Their maternalism and commitment to a social purity defined as sexual self-control had made women's organizations hesitant to declare themselves in favour of birth control; now they acknowledged its pressing need. Leftist movements and organized labour gave roughly equal support to the contradictory views that workers should rightfully decide the size of their families, and that contraception was a capitalist attempt at social control and a bourgeois practice that deprived workers of the joys of large families. Without entirely reconciling these opposing stands, labour, leftist, and farm organizations expressed outrage that the wealthy could buy access to medical advice and contraceptives, while the poor continued to have children they could not feed. Activists demanded that the state establish free birth-control clinics. The minister of health responded, not untypically, that birth control was 'a cancer that is sapping the very lifeblood of our society.'

While the eugenics movement was reaching its nightmarish pinnacle in Nazi Germany's plans to exterminate the 'unfit,' there was a brief but important resurgence of eugenic campaigns in Canada. Eugenicists in the Canadian medical profession used their social influence and expertise to encourage legislation permitting the forcible sterilization of the mentally ill, and those loosely classified as 'feeble-minded,' in British Columbia and Alberta. Women's groups such as the National Council of Women of Canada (NCWC) also supported this 'scientific' approach to human reproduction.

Often the 'sub-normal' were simply the poor, who appeared both 'unfit' and anti-social to those equally fearful of revolution and state responsibility for the needy. Unmarried pregnant women were readily targeted by eugenicists, their 'moral lassitude' interpreted as direct evidence of 'feeble-mindedness.'

As a service to his own laid-off employees, industrialist A.R. Kaufman established the Parents' Information Bureau in Kitchener, Ontario, in 1930. Kaufman was convinced that only birth control could prevent social disorder. His perspective was shared by A.H. Tryer, a retired Anglican minister who started the Birth Control Society of Canada in 1931. Their views about the urgent need to control the reproduction of the 'irresponsible classes' not only meshed with eugenicist aims, but also struck responsive chords in beleaguered municipalities struggling to maintain the families of the unemployed. Local women's organizations received Kaufman's financial support for the first birth-control clinics in Hamilton, Toronto, and Windsor. At the Hamilton clinic, a doctor counselled women and fitted diaphragms for a $3 fee. The fee was waived for those on relief, or roughly half the clients. Kaufman ultimately decided that he could reach more families cheaply and effectively through home visits and follow-up direct mailings of spermidical jelly and condoms. By the late 1930s, up to 75 bureau employees were travelling around Ontario, earning $1.00 to $1.50 commission per client, and making approximately 20,000 new contacts each year. The bureau's female workers, many of whom were trained nurses, gave out free information and arranged for the distribution of contraceptives across the country – exclusively to married women.

Bureau worker Dorothea Palmer's efforts in the predominantly Catholic francophone suburb of Eastview (outside Ottawa) led to tremendous publicity for the birth-control cause. In 1936, Palmer was tried on charges of contravening the law that prohibited distribution of contraceptive information and devices. Twenty-one women testified that they had consented to receive the bureau's package of three condoms, a tube of contraceptive jelly, and a French-language brochure. A doctor called to the stand repeated the medical line of opposition, even while admitting that the abortion rate was high, and that abortion could be avoided if contraceptives were used. The Crown proclaimed that contraception undermined traditional patriarchal authority, therefore the family itself. In a thirteen-hour testimony, the defence's key witness, the Reverend Claris Edwin Silcox, secretary of the Christian Social Council, countered that family limitation would reduce marital breakdown by allowing physical, emotional, and financial relief from the pressures of procreative sexuality. The alternative was acceptance of communism or socialism. Cast in terms of threats to family and system, and in the language of moral and religious duty, his arguments effectively contested those of the Crown. Palmer was acquitted on the grounds that her work, in promoting safe and effective birth control, served the public good. It appeared that the existing law did not reflect the real views of Canadians on the issue of family limitation. While the law remained in force for another thirty years, the Eastview trial made the birth-control movement more respectable, and prosecution less likely.

The Domestic Antidote: Theories and Policies

Dominated by the McGill School of Social Research, the sociology of the family that developed during the interwar years was premised on an evolutionary process called the 'transfer of functions,' or the socialization of reproduction. Sociologists maintained that families could no longer make it on their own in an increasingly complex and interrelated socioeconomic order. Moreover, external agencies and experts were gradually invading the family, the ultimate sanctum of privacy, and expropriating its final exclusive function, that of parenting. This process was depicted in positive terms: the community, as represented by these agents and agencies, would help the family sustain its loving internal ties by taking on some of its 'work' of social reproduction. The objective was social equilibrium through family harmony, since the family was the primary generator of shared values, order, and consensus.

Although the state still played a very limited role in this area, the professionalization of child welfare was largely accomplished during the 1930s, as childhood drew increasingly specialized attention. In the midst of economic desolation, the 'normal child' aroused new hopes and fears. Social critics, reformers, family experts, politicians, and parents worried aloud about the long-term effects of early childhood insecurity and familial instability, not only for individual famiies, but, more important, for the nation. Child behaviour became a legitimate area of medical investigation just as child psychology was developing as a distinct field, and there was much inter-borrowing between medicine and psychology. Child-welfare crusaders never wavered from their goal of national regeneration through the training of model citizens, nor from their dedication to the state intervention that they believed essential to that end. Their arguments simply became more emphatic during the 1930s.

Those who promoted the 'modern family' had to change their script, even if their solutions remained the same. Where formerly the keywords had been efficiency and productivity, a vehement defence of capitalism when it was clearly faltering was no longer altogether convincing. During the 1930s, parent education was geared to social stability. Always an important objective, it became the foremost goal, as the long-threatened crisis materialized. Family experts argued that 'arbitrary methods' employed by disheartened parents would introduce dissonant values to a new generation. Although individualism and democracy continued to be paraded as essential 'Canadian' values, social conformity was promoted as the ultimate goal. 'Traditional' childrearing methods were believed to contradict modern ideas of pacifism and equal rights. Corporal punishment, it was argued, engendered an acceptance of violence that rationalized wars, strikes, riots, crime, and all manner of civil disobedience. Parents were to be consistently firm and authoritative, but they were not to expect 'enforced and rigid obedience,' which would only lead to rebellion, deceit, even moral abdication. This view of the darker side of obedience indicates the fear of mass revolt that so disturbed the middle class, receiving new emphasis as the world witnessed the enforcement of dictatorial rule in the fascist states of Europe. European studies published in the mid-1930s linked patriarchal authoritarianism and the development of personalities prone to totalitarianism.

The best approach to childrearing, as one psychologist argued, involved the sort of careful parental regulation that allowed behaviour to be 'adjusted to social customs and practices.' The experts seemed unaware that they were, paradoxically, making conformity the only safeguard against totalitarianism. They were convinced that adherence to certain conventions was a choice freely made by educated citizens. They also contended that parent education would console economically distressed families: parents could focus on the intangible benefits of a 'good home environment,' rather than dwelling on their inability to supply an abundance of material goods for their children. As a social worker explained, the mother's 'irritability and preoccupation' and the father's 'loss of grip and sense of futility' would react badly on children, making them 'thin and nervy.' Parents had to consider the well-being of their families first, whatever their own anxieties and resentments.

Changes in the nature and content of childrearing literature from the 1920s to the 1930s demonstrate that the 'modern' concept of childrearing was more than a product of emerging medical and psychological theories. It was an evolving system of values grounded in existing class relations and the new social realities of post–First World War Canada. Physicians, psychologists, social workers, and educators theorized that parental management of the child's physical nurture was inseparable from its training for emotional and social 'fitness.' Mothers would first learn the fundamentals of physical care, then progress to correct ways of cultivating obedience, honesty, and courtesy, and coping with fears and anger. They would also learn how to foster intellectual development, moral acuity, independence, and good work habits in their children. By charging mothers with all this responsibility for the child's emotional and physical health, cognitive growth, and civic worth, experts were devising a system that made childrearing an ever more consuming process for any mother who tried to comply.

Modern childrearing was also an increasingly inflexible, mechanistic process. In their popular 1930 manual *The Management of Young Children*, pioneering Canadian child psychologists William Blatz and Helen Bott argued that 'consistent adherence to a few simple rules without any deviation whatever will permit the child to learn to make adequate social adjustments.' During the 1930s, the scientific childrearing message reached more parents than ever, thanks to continued mass circulation of free advice literature by state and private agencies. But its urban, white, middle-class perspective, the tenacity of ethnic and cultural patterns in family life, and the pressing material concerns of so many families restricted the implementation of the advice that it carried into the nation's homes. Even among families where more direct and forceful attempts at regulation were being made, the results were not as the experts hoped. The Inuit, increasingly exposed to the 'Canadianizing' influences of missionaries, doctors, nurses, and state agents during these years, were largely impervious to attempts to 'systematize' their family relations. Much to the chagrin of 'Canadian' observers, their family mealtimes and bedtimes continued to be irregular. Children ate in whatever home they wished, and were generally believed to be the best judges of their own needs and interests. The absence of discipline was not an absence of socialization, but the persistence of their traditional childrearing culture, which avoided manipulation and authoritarian treatment of the young.

Both popular currents in childrearing and the state's position on families are exemplified in the strange and sad case of the Dionne quintuplets, easily the most famous Canadian babies of all time. In 1934, the Ontario government declared itself the true parent of the infant Dionnes, who were born into a large rural family of francophone Catholics in Corbeil, near North Bay. Despite the arguments presented to the public, the Dionnes were not dealt with as children in need of state protection; they were natural resources or 'scenic wonders,' to be managed for public benefit more than their own. The infants were kept across the road from the family farm in a custom-built hospital. They were tended with the latest medical technology, and received round-the-clock nursing care, and regular supervision by the pre-eminent medical and psychological specialists of the day. With its hospital and souvenir shops, 'Quintland' soon drew as many tourists as Niagara Falls – some 400,000 in 1938 alone – offering vacationing middle-class families a glimpse of thoroughly modern babies in a quaintly rustic setting.

None of the experts involved in the quints' care, including famous paediatrician Alan Brown, and famous child psychologist William Blatz, expressed any qualms about the long-term effects of such a public upbringing. The performative aspects of their regimen, and the children's effective institutionalization and separation from family, were never regarded in any negative light. When the quints' tourist value wore off and they were returned to their parents, the latter were unable and, more important, unwilling to modify their personal childrearing values, rooted in rural French-Canadian and Catholic tradition. The results were the quints' tragic alienation from their parents, the emotional difficulties that they encountered as adults, and the sorrow and public humiliation of the elder Dionnes. No other children in Canada – perhaps anywhere – were raised as meticulously 'by the book' as they were. The Dionnes became the representative ideal of 1930s childhood, but they were deprived of anything remotely like an ideal childhood themselves.

Another Lost Generation: 'Idle Youth'

One reason why the official statistics barely tell the story of the Depression's human casualties is that those most affected were those who came of age in the 1930s, had never previously held full-time wage work, and consequently did not show up in the numbers. At the life-stage that would ordinarily have found them pursuing higher education or vocational training, commencing work, marrying, and setting up households, young people were being forced into a sort of waiting zone. The 1930s witnessed growing fears that young Canadians would become the particular victims of disillusionment, a ready audience for subversive ideologies such as communism, and related 'immoral practices' that spelled doom for the family. For many observers, 'the moral result' was the most serious effect of prolonged youth unemployment. Editorials in *Social Welfare*, official journal of the Social Service Council, pointed out that, instead of finding the 'gateways of opportunity and paths of honourable service' available to previous generations, young people were facing 'the wall of blank negation that can neither be climbed nor cast down.' Writing in *Maclean's* in 1934, one young woman felt that she spoke for her generation when she declared that 'our sense of values is slipping – we condone today what we condemned yesterday.' Young Canadians were losing faith in their leaders and the future of their country. She wondered whether the time had come for a 'complete revolt against old traditions – traditions which seem to have failed not only the older people, but youth as well.'

Alarmed Canadians argued that the situation of 'idle youth' was a national emergency, much more pressing than concerns about the reckless frivolity of the previous decade's 'flaming youth.' The only rational preventive measures appeared to be the postponement of unemployment through extended schooling, and the provision of healthful pastimes to steer young people away from the more destructive variety that inevitably led to sexual licence, juvenile delinquency, or radical politics. The Council on Child and Family Welfare warned that, left to their own devices, the young unemployed would become disaffected, seeing themselves as a class apart, 'subject to misfortunes which do not touch their fellows.' Boys were turning to street gangs to while away the time, and girls were allegedly submitting to 'moral laxity,' bartering sex for an evening out or stylish clothes. A farm family in Selkirk, Manitoba, was torn apart by one daughter's admission that her job in a Winnipeg restaurant was a cover for the prostitution that really kept her fed and 'in good clothes.' The national crisis signified the deterioration of proper social relations, and the family values at their core.

The problem of 'idle youth' thus replaced that of 'flaming youth' during the Depression. As the Young Men's Christian Association's national council pointed out, various anti-democratic movements around the world were mobilizing unemployed youth and exploiting the potential power for social change that this 'strategic mass group' possessed. In view of that growing danger, it was both 'economical and safe to conserve a source of future good citizenship.' On one hand, there was much guilt and apprehension about the Depression's impact on young Canadians. On the other, there was a sense that it might serve as a necessary lesson for extravagant and irresponsible youth after the high times of the Roaring Twenties. It would teach them the benefits of family life and active community participation, breaking the insidious hold of immoral and amoral commercialized amusements. In the home, and in community-sponsored and supervised activities, the young would learn democratic ideals, the value of education, collective social responsibility, conventions respecting sexuality, and, according to the YMCA and many like-minded youth organizations, 'the worth of religion as a workable philosophy of life.'

Whatever the arguments for productive, and regulated, use of their idle hours, the young unemployed were facing adulthood without any prospects for paid work and independence from their families. Municipal relief was largely denied to them, and they were now an extra burden, where previously they would have been able to contribute to their own upkeep, perhaps even setting out on their own. Some 70,000 young Canadian men hit the road during the 1930s, travelling across the country in empty boxcars, meeting with hostility everywhere they stopped, frequently encountering the indifference, if not the brute force, of the authorities. The predicted crime wave never materialized. The single unemployed were more a menace to public health than to public safety or even morality. Four thousand destitute men, mostly transients, lived in Vancouver's 'hobo jungles' in shacks made of bits of tin and wood, old car bodies, discarded signs, and scraps. Vancouverites saw them sleeping in the rain among rats and foraging alongside them for remnants of food. The government's preventative measure against contagious diseases such as typhoid, and contagious ideologies such as communism, was to place them in work camps under the direction of the armed forces. By June 1933, these camps were operating in every province but Prince Edward Island.During the 3 1/2 years of the camps' existence, 170,000 men passed through them. Inmates laboured forty-four hours per week on construction and clearing projects for a twenty-cent daily allowance, plus shelter, clothing, food, and medical care. Those over the age of majority were disenfranchised. There were strict codes of behaviour, and nothing, no reading material, recreational equipment, or organized activities, to fill leisure hours. Those who left the camps voluntarily were denied any further relief. Although provided for in the material sense, relief camp inmates, in the words of one, were 'truly a lost legion of youth.'

Regarded as more subordinate and superfluous than unemployed men, single women were in an even more precarious position. In the early 1930s, relief in any form was still withheld from unemployed single women. In Vancouver their desperate straits prompted the establishment of women's hostels by local charity organizations. When city relief was finally granted in early 1933, it remained difficult for single women to qualify. Many had to take domestic-service positions for as little as five dollars per month, sometimes with room and board in lieu of wages. Relief was granted only if domestic service were unavailable, or because of ill health. It usually took the form of meal and bed tickets that obliged them to give up their own lodgings and stay in designated hotels. Theirs was a 'waste heritage,' as characterized by contemporary author Irene Baird in her novel detailing the lives of young Canadians during the Great Depression.

Enter the State – Reluctantly

Municipal and provincial governments became increasingly involved in health and welfare during the opening decades of the twentieth century. Except for the war emergency, however, the federal government had largely managed to remain aloof. Constitutional complications, fiscal conservatism, and a commitment to local care of the poor and sick had kept most federal initiatives on behalf of families firmly in the realm of public education and rhetorical support. In overturning the family lives of many Canadians, the Depression also dramatically affected the state's role in them. It widened public recognition of the federal government's obligation to protect Canadians against the economic risks, such as unemployment, that are intrinsic to industrial capitalism. Eventually, political lessons learned during the Depression would change the relationship between families and the state.

For the first half of the decade, few effective federal measures were taken in the face of mass distress. Programs attempting to address the plight of families were often rooted in a nostalgic 'rural myth,' explaining much of the current situation as the direct result of heedless migration to urban industrial areas. In 1931 the federal cabinet proposed a scheme to use relief funds from all three levels of government to establish the unemployed on self-supporting farms – seemingly oblivious to the fact that already-established farm families were enduring great hardship. The Nova Scotia government expropriated 600 vacant farms in 1932, granting them to the families of the unemployed, chiefly those of miners. By 1938, more than one-third had abandoned their farms; another third were behind in payments; only twenty-four of the original families fulfilled the conditions giving them title to their land. Initial enthusiasm was also great when New Brunswick decided to participate by opening new lands to settlement. With the full endorsement of a Catholic clergy which had traditionally supported colonization to offset out-migration, the Acadian community sent about 600 of its families per year to settle the northern counties, a total of about 11,165 settlers by 1939. Federal and provincial surveys on the dozen or so new communities then in existence described them as impoverished rural slums, lacking in basic services and amenities, with few self-supporting families and high rates of illiteracy.

The Quebec Liberal government likewise revived its ill-fated colonization movement, initially established in 1916. Assisted by clergy, nationalists, and farmers' organizations, the Taschereau administration urged Quebeckers to turn 'back to the land,' where large families, the Catholic faith, and the agrarian vocation would ensure the survival of 'la nation.' To emphasize that this was a project of family regeneration as well as economic and national renewal, applicants (male) had to be legally married, and had to agree to settle a plot of land with only their families. Their wives had to know how to sew, knit, perform all household duties, and make bread. The emphasis placed on the marital/familial status of the colonist and the domestic skills of his wife acknowledged the vital contribution of families to agricultural success. It also confirmed the importance of traditional gender and domestic roles as measures of moral commitment to a francophone, Catholic society. The new Action Liberale Nationale party, formed in 1934 and later coopted into Maurice Duplessis's conservative Union Nationale, also equated economic recovery with rural recovery based on the family farm. Elected in

1936 with the support of the Church and many among the nationalist elite, the Union Nationale's own plans for social restoration glorified this 'return to the land' and the large, industrious, devout, rural French-Catholic family.

The penalties of ageing were made harsher by the Depression, as children and other kin were increasingly unable to help elderly Canadians. Applications to charity and to old-age refuges for the indigent increased greatly. Recognizing that skyrocketing relief expenditures made their participation expedient, previously reluctant provincial governments were now persuaded to take advantage of the federal Old Age Pensions program of 1927, which was based on shared fiscal responsibility with the provinces. The federal contribution was set at 75 per cent in 1931, again enhancing the appeal of this shared responsibility for those over the age of seventy years. Faced with a disproportionate number of elderly, the Maritimes still lacked the finances to implement the program on any but a minimal level. The Prince Edward Island scheme introduced in 1933 allowed only one in five of those over seventy to qualify, and its pensions were less than 60 per cent of those paid in Ontario and western Canada. Nova Scotia adopted a similar plan in 1934, New Brunswick in 1936. In Ontario, as the number of pension applications grew with increasing unemployment among both the elderly and the offspring who could reasonably support them, there were attempts to make 'base ingrates'– children who forced their parents onto the pension rolls – do their duty. After 1932, the ability of children to contribute to their upkeep was counted as income, regardless whether they actually did. The amount was deducted from the annual ceiling of $365 – one dollar per day – even if the elderly parents never saw one cent of it.

Woman-headed families frequently saw their already-scant provisions further pared down. Relief officials stepped up attempts to prosecute deserting husbands and enforce child support in order to prevent misallocation of scarce public funds. Locating deserters was futile when so many of them were unemployed; even the law could not make them provide. The Depression exposed the plight of thousands of needy mothers and children, especially those with only one child, who were excluded from mothers' allowance provisions by rigid eligiblity requirements at a time when they could not find work. An Ontario widow, an invalid with a sick nine-year-old child and parents on relief, sent an impassioned plea to Liberal premier Mitch Hepburn: 'to raise a future Canadian in the way he should be raised is an important and full-time job, enough responsibility for any woman however strong, without the added burden of trying to find a job and keeping it.' Beginning in 1934, the age of eligibility was extended to children up to eighteen years if they remained in school. Shortly thereafter, widows with one child were permitted benefits. The period of desertion, or 'unknown whereabouts' of the deserting husband, was reduced from five to three years in response to the unemployment crisis. By 1939, the program supported more than 12,000 Ontario families, four times the amount supported in the early 1920s. Benefits, however, amounted to a mere $28 monthly per family, a sum that the Mothers' Allowance Commission was forced to admit was insufficient.

In light of the well-received attempt by U.S. president Franklin D. Roosevelt to encourage economic recovery through a 'New Deal,' Prime Minister Bennett conjured up his own version in 1935. The Bennett New Deal intended sweeping welfare reform, but its linchpin unemployment-insurance scheme excluded about 40 per cent of all wage-earners. Most of its remaining measures were outside federal jurisdiction, and consequently unconstitutional. By mid-decade, dissatisfaction with existing politics spawned new parties on both left (Cooperative Commonwealth Federation) and right (Social Credit). Under the leadership of preacher and teacher William Aberhart, Social Credit became Alberta's government in 1935 on the promise of a $25 monthly dividend paid to each family. No family ever saw any such payment. The social-democratic CCF, which evolved from the labour–farmer coalition of the Progressive movement, was instrumental in pressuring provincial governments to improve relief measures. For his part, Mackenzie King performed little differently than Bennett upon succeeding him as prime minister in December 1935. King's Liberal administration refused to define any national minimum standard; instead it defined a national maximum in 1937. At a time when few provinces had legislated minimum wages, the standard of living on relief had to be kept below that attainable on the average wages of unskilled labour in each area. The despised work camps were replaced with a farm placement scheme which paid about 45,000 single unemployed men five dollars per month to work on farms across the country. This amounted to even less than the infamous twenty cents daily allowance, and now without guaranteed adequate food, clothing, shelter, and medical care.

Most of the King government's attempts to 'solve' the relief question took the form of investigation. King appointed a National Employment Commission in April 1936 to recommend reforms of the unemployment and relief structures. In August 1937 he also established the pivotal Royal Commission on Dominion–Provincial Relations to untangle the mess of jurisdictional questions that the crisis had brought to the fore. Both finished on the same note. Reporting in January 1938 and May 1940, respectively, the commissions proposed that Ottawa initiate a national employment service and system of unemployment insurance and assume total financial and administrative responsibility for unemployment relief. Echoed by many influential Canadians, King's personal view was that such a plan would be too expensive and would erode the work ethic, contributing to further unemployment and dependence on the state – the traditional bogey of 'pauperization.'

In the absence of a sustained, united threat from leftist movements and organized labour, public pressure was simply not sufficient to allow for state intervention in the degree that circumstances seemed to require. The Second World War, with the full employment it would bring – for the first time ever for many Canadians – and re-energized labour organization, permitted the instigation of structural reforms to underpin the incomes of the working poor, and to provide for the dependent. The ironies did not escape working-class Canadians. A sardonic poem in *The Labour Leader* in 1938 foresaw immediately improved prospects for families once the state was obliged to invest in the war that already appeared inevitable. In 'Owed to the Future,' a 'Veteran of Future Wars,' currently unemployed, is finally able to marry and start a family on the 'tidy little sum' to be provided by his 'Future Soldier's Bonus for the War That's Yet to Come.' With the coming of war and the full employment and state economic management that resulted, the Great Depression of ten years' duration finally ended. Another crisis in the family had been weathered.

Conclusion

Dire predictions to the contrary, the Great Depression did not bring about the family's demise. Yet families had to deal with considerable stresses and strains during the 1930s, not only economically, but also respecting their relations with each other and the outside world. In many homes, the Depression compelled a dramatic, if temporary, readjustment of roles and functions. Men not only lost their essential provider role, and perhaps their sense of rightful authority within the family – the underpinnings of manliness – but also their work routine, and so, for many, the very form and textures of their lives. Women working outside the home also had to deal with new routines, but their identity as wives and mothers did not depend so much on the actual labour that they performed. It could be that women who did not go out to work felt the disruption more, as husbands traditionally held dominance while present in the home. Now they were present all the time, perhaps only as involuntary spectators of a domestic scene to which they may have been ill-equipped to contribute.

Other family members found their individual life- courses profoundly affected. Many children could no longer count on a childhood removed as much as possible from adult responsibilities. Many were kept home from school for lack of food and clothing. Adolescents were trapped in a limbo of frustrated expectations. Young women became virtual prisoners in their parents' homes. Young men, whom society allowed other options, took to the streets, 'rode the rails,' or submitted to military law in the 'relief camps' established to contain another lost generation. And the prospect of indigence, always close enough for many of the elderly, now threatened their security more than ever before.

The most significant effect for families was the widespread material insecurity that shook many of those in classes and regions formerly protected from the worst impact of economic jolts. A result of this was the widening commitment among the reform-minded, many now organized under the aegis of the Cooperative Commonwealth Federation, to define a social minimum beneath which no Canadian citizen would ever be allowed to sink, and to support that minimum through state intervention. The reforms that actually came forward during the Depression years were limited, serving more as a political bridge to the welfare legislation of the Second World War and Reconstruction, when the King government was at last prepared to introduce coherent, national social security measures. Unemployment insurance became a reality in 1941. Leonard Marsh's *Report on Social Security for Canada*, presented to the House of Commons Committee on Reconstruction and Rehabilitation in 1943, attempted to establish a justifiable social minimum, proclaiming that children 'should have an unequivocal place in social security policy.' After much criticism and consternation, the Family Allowances Act was passed in 1944. These were universal programs extended to all Canadians, in contrast to the needs-based measures of the interwar years.

Unemployment insurance and family allowances marked the most unequivocal entry by the Canadian state into the sphere of social reproduction. Without disputing the desirability and value of these measures, both were inarguably significant reinforcements for the system. They were intended to mitigate class conflict, bolster the male breadwinner, and maintain the spending power of families through the consumer-housewife. However modern their depiction, they also upheld the traditional family ethic and the traditional view of male and female roles, in both the home and the marketplace. The federal government would assist families in their reproductive activities and care of non-working members, while assuring women's role in maintaining and reproducing the labour force, thereby institutionalizing its pattern of intervention in the family. Women, in fact, were mostly ineligible for unemployment-insurance benefits.

The Second World War brought its own set of problems for families, but it also gave rise to the most domestically oriented generation of young Canadians that the twentieth century would know. Those who survived these years of economic and military emergency would reinstitute a version of the cult of domesticity that prevailed a century earlier, actually setting off a 'baby boom' in their renewed commitment to 'the family.' Once Canadians resettled themselves after the second global conflict of the century, many would happily go home to a family that at least looked like the family of middle-class ideal 'in process' since the middle of the previous century – despite such changes as the decline in family size, 'scientific' approaches to childrearing, new expectations about companionate marriage and sexual compatibility, and somewhat more lenient divorce laws. The Depression may have slowed earlier steps taken towards the modern family – the sheltered childhood, the 'new morality,' companionate marriage, the idealization of the male-breadwinner model – but the setback would prove temporary.

Conclusion:
The Infinite Bonds of Family,
1850–1940

To return to our metaphor, several 'punctuation' points shook Canadian families at certain moments over the course of the near-century between 1850 and 1940, unsettling the lives of individual family members as well as that of the group, and obliging them to find ways to restore equilibrium. Each, in turn, sparked structural changes that were met by familial adaptations. In addition to jolting families in their own way, the Industrial Revolution, the Great War, and the Great Depression accelerated trends that moved families incrementally, along a jagged path, to a recognizably 'modern' form by the middle of the twentieth century. Rather than focusing on the immediate impact of such historic events, we would do better to understand their repercussions in terms of the ongoing process of family change during these years.

Structural and familial change are so entwined that it is difficult to see which initiates change in the other, and which responds, in any given moment. What we can identify with a little more certainty are the major influences working to reconfigure domestic relations in Canada during these years. Four of these stand out: economic changes, particularly the shift from domestic to factory production; demographic changes, especially the decline in family size; changes in the socio-economic status of women; and the changing relations between the private sphere, represented by 'the family,' and the public interest increasingly represented by the state.

First, industrialization, and the related forces of urbanization and immigration, were having recognizable transformative effects on both the new Dominion of Canada and its families by the closing quarter of the nineteenth century. In colonial British North America, families were interdependent economic units focused on familial prosperity and inheritance. Most production was family-based and located in the household, as were the education of children, the transmission of skills, and the care of the elderly, the infirm, and those otherwise dependent. The economic changes commencing by mid-century saw the eventual transfer of many of these customary familial functions to outside institutions. Work became identified with wage labour that was usually performed outside of the home, primarily by men.

Nineteenth-century public discourses idealized specific gender-defined roles in private and public spheres. Women and children, however, continued to participate actively in working-class and farm family economies, though increasingly through 'informal,' unpaid but still important contributions. Middle-class women gradually became managers of household consumption. Children, more and more removed from production, became economic dependants requiring significant parental investment in their welfare. Parental, especially paternal, authority declined, as parents were less able to provide for their children's futures through inherited property, trades, or businesses. The family's role as material provider for its members continued, but its major public purpose was redefined in terms of emotional more than material sustenance, of preparation for citizenship rather than specific skills training. The preindustrial family serving public needs was slowly being replaced by a more 'private' type of family that performed more specialized reproductive functions. Paradoxically, this privatized family became more susceptible than ever to public scrutiny and intervention, as the socialization of children, and the regulation of domestic relations, came to be regarded as critical components of national welfare.

Aboriginal families were probably most dramatically affected by this conjuncture of social and familial change. Their traditional family economies based on hunting, trapping, and fishing, and their economic, social, and political customs derived from kin relations, were increasingly subjected to the interference of missionaries, traders, government agents, and white settlers. The latter also became critical of 'mixed' marriages, and more forceful in imposing European notions about the patriarchal family. By mid-century, Aboriginal and Métis women were no longer sought as 'country wives' of traders. Their offspring, known as 'half-breeds' or Métis, depending upon their British or French-Canadian paternity, constituted a whole new society recognized by successive post-Confederation governments as neither 'Canadian' nor 'Status Indian.' The reserve system and the forced transition to a settled farming lifestyle were the intended outcome of late-nineteenth-century land treaties. By the turn of the century, many Native families were living on impoverished reserves, suffering spiritually and bodily from their confinement, and facing a mounting threat of deculturation through Euro-Canadian educational, economic, and domestic institutions.

Second, the changing form and nature of Canadian families were at once cause and effect of demographic developments, as conscious choices led to a decline in fertility and a reduction in family size. Colonial farm couples began to limit their families to deal with the shortage of good land that was affecting familial prospects. From about the middle of the nineteenth century, women were giving birth less often, spacing children more closely, and reaching an earlier end to childbearing. By the end of the nineteenth century, it was unusual for women to continue bearing children into their forties. The 1871 census showed an average of five children per family; by 1921, the average number was three.

Another critical demographic change was the gradual extension of life expectancy, although the class basis of much ill health made its impact variable. Infant mortality, deficiency diseases, and tuberculosis remained serious problems among the working poor. Native Canadians actually saw their population decline until the 1930s. Nonetheless, in general terms, infant mortality was reduced, various state and voluntary agencies began making inroads into public-health problems, and improvements in medical diagnostics and therapeutics helped at least those who had access to a doctor's care. Finally, a related demographic trend was the gradual ageing of society. For a growing proportion of Canadians, whole new life-stages would open up as a result: a period of marriage after the childrearing stage, a longer relationship with adult children, grandparenthood, and prolonged widowhood – all with implications for marital relations, family responsibilities, and economic dependence, especially for women, who were statistically more likely to be widowed.

The third important marker of family change relates to the role and status of Canadian women, and their traditional primary identification with family. By mid-nineteenth century, the ideal family was predicated on the central, almost sacred, notion of complementary but distinct 'spheres' defined by a gendered division of labour. The system rested on a conceptual separation of female reproductive and male productive activities. With the growing separation of work and home, wage labour and domestic production, the chief duties of middle-class wives came to be associated with the maintenance of the home as a refuge from the chaos of industrial society, and the moral influence that they were to exert on children and husbands alike. For Aboriginal women, amendments to the Indian Act legislated subordination, patrilineage, the primacy of reproduction, and their exclusive identification according to the 'Indian' status of their husbands.

Just as the 'proper sphere' of women was increasingly confined to hearth and home, new opportunities were presenting themselves. Ideals notwithstanding, women of all classes were making choices and living lives that did not always fit public notions about their proper sphere. The 'woman question' came to be equated with the crisis in the family, as greater numbers of women worked before marriage, attained higher levels of formal schooling, deliberately limited the size of their families, or eschewed marriage and motherhood altogether. The Great War accelerated these trends towards feminine autonomy and delivered political rights. These developments implied both a 'new day' for women and the beginnings of a 'new morality' that threatened to liberate feminine sexuality. It appears that Canadians were frightened enough by the prospects alone. The result was a conservative backlash that aimed to bring about social regeneration through a politics of maternalism.

The fourth notable trend involves the increasing intervention of authorities in the family, usually in the form of 'experts' drawn from the 'helping professions' of medicine, social work, psychology, and education, and often from state agencies. After the Great War, a host of family-centred reformers constructed a modern ideal of family life: the companionate family, ruled by affection, mutual respect, and shared authority. They reasoned that the perceived 'crisis in the family' was caused by a 'vacuum of authority,' amounting to nothing less than a crisis in patriarchy. The void could not be filled by the traditional patriarch, who, while retaining his symbolic power, was now above all the chief breadwinner. Nor would the traditional sources of guidance found in kin, community, and church suffice in this complex modern age. The modern family would find its way by following the lead of qualified family experts, and the state would see that childrearing became modern and scientific. The newly professionalized modern mother would equip her children to fit neatly into the productive, efficient society that was the ideal modern Canada.

While it is evident that not all Canadians accepted either the new model or the resultant new relationship with experts and agencies, it is also clear that deviant or 'problem' families were measured against these ideals, and policy made accordingly. Governments took their cues from the new experts in health, education, and social welfare, and participated in various campaigns intended to supervise, regulate, and 'educate' families into modern citizenship. As they defined it, this was a narrow brand of citizenship derived from the white, middle-class, Protestant, Anglo-Celtic model of their own experiences. Their domestic ideals were carried into homes by visiting nurses, social workers, doctors, family court personnel, mothers' allowance supervisors, teachers, and any number of volunteers involved in community welfare projects. Reformers intended that the state should bolster the patriarchal family, complementing and supplementing the steadily diminishing protective role of the father. But the state's form of protection most often took the shape of regulation, involving a certain invasion of, and interference in, the private family – though all in its own best interests, and for the national good.

For families that could not, or would not accept the model, the price for any tangible benefits was likely high. Children of immigrants may have found themselves distanced from their families by their teachers' and social workers' insistence on Anglo-conformity. Aboriginal families were damaged by the removal of children to distant residential schools, where many suffered physical and emotional abuse in addition to cultural alienation. Single-parent families were virtually placed under guard by mothers' allowance commissioners and suspicious neighbours. 'Ignorant' mothers of all origins were subjected to a barrage of childrearing advice and supervision that, while not unappreciated, was nonetheless limited in achieving improved health and family lives when these were so often contingent on material circumstances. The gap between the ideal model and reality became painfully evident during the Great Depression, when deprivations finally undermined much of the historic resistance to state welfarism.

The configurations of family that evolved with these unfolding trends between 1850 and 1940 – two vastly different Canadas – demonstrate significant continuities, despite the very things that made them, each in turn, new models. There were two constants throughout this entire period: the perception that 'the family' was in crisis; and the belief that the best solution was adherence to a family model based on a gender-defined male-breadwinner ideal. Where the latter is concerned, the real and the ideal were edging closer by the end of the 1920s. The Great Depression proved a potent setback. For most Canadians, the ideal was elusive, if not impossible, until the improved material conditions, and the corresponding 'family wage,' were realized with the Second World War and its prosperous aftermath. Fitting domestic reality to ideal was something that took place slowly, incrementally, and contingently. The timing, and ultimately the closeness of the fit, were greatly affected by class, occupational status of the male head of household, geographic region, ethnic background, and race.   But the ideal was obviously sufficiently important to enough Canadians to have never been given up. Post–Second World War affluence, the 'baby boom,' and the resurgence of 'traditional' family values in an essentially conservative ideological climate saw the 'new domesticity' well entrenched by the mid-1950s, even as this view of the norm continued to marginalize a substantial number of families.

In spite of adaptations to circumstances internal and external, and in spite of new paradigms, the power relations governing the family dynamic remained essentially unchanged. The dominant class established the 'norm,' and regulated and punished those who deviated from it, increasingly with the support of the state. Familial power relations – the internal subordination imposed by gender and age – likewise persisted. The politics of family have always included subordination and coercion, largely age- and gender-defined. Behind its idealized representation – what Karl Marx aptly called 'the sentimental veil'– the family can mask dysfunctional relationships leading to the abuse and exploitation of its most vulnerable members. At the same time, however, families continue to offer invaluable, often irreplaceable, sources of nurture and emotional sustenance, mutuality, and reciprocity.

However the current wave of 'family crisis' was perceived, social observers consistently argued that the welfare of family, society, and state were inextricable. These were the bonds that were truly infinite. Just as we continue to do now, they paid little attention to previous episodes of family 'crisis.' Each generation of family-watchers denies any historical memory, and casts its own version as a completely new development threatening the stability of mythical 'traditional' families as never before. Anxious preoccupation with the condition and prospects of 'the family,' therefore, is as persistent – and as infinite in form and nature – as are families themselves. Heading towards the twenty-first century, 'the crisis in the family' continues to set off waves of public debate, media obsession, and mass anxiety. Most Canadians, meanwhile, continue to find some notion of family important to their own histories, and meaningful in their own lives.

Select Bibliography

Introduction: Thinking Historically about Canadian Families

Among the best-known examples of the demographic approach are the pioneering efforts by Michael Katz, *The People of Hamilton, Canada West: Family and Class in a Mid-Nineteenth Century City* (Cambridge, Mass.: Harvard University Press, 1975), and David Gagan, *Hopeful Travellers: Families, Land and Social Change in Mid-Victorian Peel County, Canada West* (Toronto: Ontario Historical Studies Series, 1981). This approach has been particularly influential in Quebec, where parish records are more plentiful and detailed, as suggested by Gérard Bouchard, *Quelques arpents d'Amérique.* (Montreal: Boréal, 1995). Bettina Bradbury's studies of late-nineteenth-century working-class families in Montreal, culminating in *Working Families: Age, Gender and Daily Survival in Industrializing Montreal* (Toronto: McClelland & Stewart, 1992), effectively combine life-course analysis and a focus on family strategies. Changing attitudes, and their reflection in new institutions and policies, are highlighted in Neil Sutherland's seminal *Children in English-Canadian Society* (Toronto: University of Toronto Press, 1976). Peter Ward details social customs and practices in *Courtship, Love and Marriage in Nineteenth-Century English Canada* (Montreal and Kingston: McGill-Queen's University Press, 1990). The respective works of James Snell, *In the Shadow of the Law: Divorce in Canada, 1900–1939* (Toronto: University of Toronto Press, 1991) and *The Citizen's Wage: The State and the Elderly in Canada, 1900–1951* (Toronto: University of

Toronto Press, 1996), Karen Dubinsky's *Improper Advances: Rape and Heterosexual Conflict in Ontario, 1880–1929* (Chicago: University of Chicago Press, 1993), and Carolyn Strange's *Toronto's Girl Problem: The Perils and Pleasures of the City, 1880–1930* (Toronto: University of Toronto Press, 1995), examine the coalescence of legal and social constructions behind changing attitudes towards marriage and divorce, the elderly, sexuality, and youth, and their impact on law and social policy. A gendered analysis, focusing on women, is featured in Veronica Strong-Boag's *The New Day Recalled: Lives of Girls and Women in English Canada, 1919–1939* (Toronto: Penguin, 1988), and Andrée Lévesque's *La Norme et les déviantes: Des femmes au Québec pendant l'entre-deux-guerres* (Montreal: Rémue-Ménage, 1989), translated by Yvonne Klein as *Making and Breaking the Rules: Women in Quebec, 1919–1939* (Toronto: McClelland & Stewart, 1994). Denyse Baillargeon's *Ménagères au temps de la Crise* (Montreal: Remue-Ménage, 1991), about working-class Montreal housewives during the Great Depression, Marilyn Porter's *Place and Persistence in the Lives of Newfoundland Women* (Brookfield, Ver.: Avebury, 1993), Katherine Arnup's *Education for Motherhood: Advice for Mothers in Twentieth-Century Canada* (Toronto: University of Toronto Press, 1994), and Neil Sutherland's *Growing Up: Childhood in English Canada from the Great War to the Age of Television* (Toronto: University of Toronto Press, 1997) all use fascinating oral testimony. In light of post-structuralist theories that emphasize how identities such as class, gender, and race are socially constructed, Joy Parr's *The Gender of Breadwinners: Women, Men, and Change in Two Industrial Towns, 1880–1950* (Toronto: University of Toronto Press, 1990) demonstrates the interrelations of class, gender, family, and community in shaping distinct work and family experiences for women and for men, even when both were wage-earners. Suzanne Morton's *Ideal Surroundings: Domestic Life in a Working-Class Suburb in the 1920s* (Toronto: University of Toronto Press, 1995) examines issues of idealized femininity, masculinity, and working-class domesticity in a Halifax neighbourhood. On state formation, state intervention, social reproduction, and welfare policy, see the inaugural study by Patricia Schnell and R.L. Rooke, *Discarding the Asylum: From Child Rescue to the Welfare State in English Canada, 1800–1950* (Lanham, Md.:

University Press of America, 1983). Historical sociologist Jane Ursel has produced the invaluable *Private Lives, Public Policy: 100 Years of State Intervention in the Family* (Toronto: Women's Press, 1992). Other works that use variations of this sociological model of social reproduction include my own *'Nations Are Built of Babies': Saving Ontario's Mothers and Children, 1900–1940* (Montreal and Kingston: McGill-Queen's University Press, 1993), Dorothy Chunn's *From Punishment to Doing Good: Family Courts and Socialized Justice in Ontario, 1880–1940* (Toronto: University of Toronto Press, 1993), and James Struthers's *The Limits of Affluence: Welfare in Ontario, 1920–1970* (Toronto: Ontario Historical Studies Series, 1994). An important collection of recent approaches to family history can be found in E.-A. Montigny and L. Chambers, eds., *Family Matters: Papers in Post-Confederation Canadian Family History* (Toronto: Scholars Press, 1998).

Chapter 1: The New Order

Axelrod, P. *The Promise of Schooling: Education in Canada, 1800–1914*. Toronto: University of Toronto Press, 1997.

Backhouse, C. *Petticoats and Prejudice: Women and Law in Nineteenth-Century Canada*. Toronto: Women's Press, 1991.

Bouchard, G. *Quelques arpents d'Amérique*. Montreal: Boréal, 1995.

Bourne, P., W. Mitchinson, P. Bristow, G. Cuthbert Brandt, B. Light, N. Black, and A. Prentice. *Canadian Women: A History*, 2d ed. Toronto: Harcourt, Brace, Jovanovich, 1995.

Bradbury, B. *Working Families: Age, Gender and Daily Survival in Industrializing Montreal*. Toronto: McClelland & Stewart, 1992.

Bristow, P. '"Whatever You Raise in the Ground You Can Sell It in Chatham": Black Women in Buxton and Chatham, 1850–65.' In *'We're Rooted Here and They Can't Pull Us Up': Essays in African Canadian Women's History*, ed. P. Bristow, D. Brand, L. Carty, Afua P. Cooper, S. Hamilton, and A. Shadd. Toronto: University of Toronto Press, 1994.

Brody, H. *The People's Land: Inuit, Whites and the Eastern Arctic*, 2d ed. Vancouver: Douglas & MacIntyre, 1991.

Brookes, A. 'Family, Youth, and Leaving Home in Late-Nineteenth- Century Rural Nova Scotia: Canning and the Exodus,

1868–1885.' In *Childhood and Family in Canadian History*, ed.
J. Parr. Toronto: McClelland & Stewart, 1983.

Brown, J. *Strangers in Blood: Fur Trade Company Families in Indian
Country*. Vancouver: University of British Columbia Press, 1980.

Bullen, J. 'Hidden Workers: Child Labour and the Family
Economy in Late Nineteenth-Century Urban Ontario.' In
Canadian Family History: Selected Readings, ed. B. Bradbury.
Toronto: Copp Clark Pitman, 1992.

Burnet, J., and H. Palmer. *'Coming Canadians': An Introduction to
a History of Canada's Peoples*. Toronto: McClelland & Stewart,
1988.

Carter, S. *Lost Harvests: Prairie Indian Reserve Farmers and Government Policy*. Montreal and Kingston: McGill-Queen's University
Press, 1990.

Chambers, L. *Married Women and Property Law in Victorian Ontario*.
Toronto: University of Toronto Press, 1997.

Clio Collective. *Quebec Women: A History*. Toronto: Women's
Press, 1987.

Conrad, M., T. Laidlaw, and D. Smyth, eds. *No Place Like Home:
Diaries and Letters of Nova Scotia Women*. Halifax: Formac, 1988.

Cuthbert Brandt, G. '"Weaving It Together": Life Cycle and the
Industrial Experience of Female Cotton Workers in Quebec,
1910–1950.' In *The Neglected Majority: Essays in Canadian
Women's History*, vol. 2, ed. A. Prentice and S. Trofimenkoff.
Toronto: McClelland & Stewart, 1991.

Errington, J. *Wives and Mothers, Schoolmistresses and Scullerymaids:
Women in Upper Canada, 1790–1840*. Montreal and Kingston:
McGill-Queen's University Press, 1995.

Fahmy-Eid, N., and M. Dumont, eds. *Maîtresses de maison,
maîtresses d'école: Femmes, familles et éducation dans l'histoire du
Québec*. Montreal: Boréal Express, 1983.

Fiske, Jo-anne. 'Carrier Women and the Politics of Mothering.'
In *British Columbia Reconsidered: Essays on Women*, ed. V. Strong-
Boag and G. Creese. Vancouver: Press Gang, 1992.

Gaffield, C. *Language, Schooling and Cultural Conflict: The Origins
of the French Language Controversy in Ontario*. Montreal and
Kingston: McGill-Queen's University Press, 1987.

Gagan, D. *Hopeful Travellers: Families, Land and Social Change in*

Mid-Victorian Peel County, Canada West. Toronto: Ontario Historical Studies Series, 1981.

Harney, R., and H. Troper. *Immigrants: A Portrait of the Urban Experience, 1890–1930.* Toronto: Van Nostrand Reinhold, 1975.

Henripin, J. *Trends and Factors of Fertility in Canada.* Ottawa: Statistics Canada, 1972.

Katz, M. *The People of Hamilton, Canada West: Family and Class in a Mid-Nineteenth Century City.* Cambridge, Mass.: Harvard University Press, 1975.

Lemieux, D., and L. Mercier. *Les femmes au tournant du siècle: 1880–1940: Âges de la vie, maternité, et quotidien.* Quebec: Institut québécois de recherche sur la culture, 1989.

Loewen, R. *Family, Church, and Market: A Mennonite Community in the Old and the New Worlds.* Toronto: University of Toronto Press, 1993.

Marks, L. *Revivals and Roller Rinks: Religion, Leisure, and Identity in Late Nineteenth-Century Small-Town Ontario.* Toronto: University of Toronto Press, 1996.

Miller, J.R. *Shingwauk's Vision: A History of Native Residential Schools.* Toronto: University of Toronto Press, 1996.

Montigny, E.A. *Foisted Upon the State? The Elderly in Nineteenth-Century Ontario.* Montreal and Kingston: McGill-Queen's University Press, 1997.

Morgan, C. *Public Men and Virtuous Women: The Gendered Languages of Religion and Politics in Upper Canada, 1791–1850.* Toronto: University of Toronto Press, 1996.

Morrison, R.B., and C. Roderick Wilson, eds. *Native Peoples: The Canadian Experience,* 2d ed. Toronto: McClelland & Stewart, 1995.

Morton, S. 'Separate Spheres in a Separate World: African–Nova Scotian Women in Late Nineteenth-Century Halifax County.' *Acadiensis* 22/2 (Spring 1992): 61–83.

Parr, J. *Labouring Children.* London: Croom Helm, 1980.

Porter, M. *Place and Persistence in the Lives of Newfoundland Women.* Brookfield, Ver.: Avebury, 1993.

Ramirez, B. *On the Move: French-Canadian and Italian Miigrants in the North Atlantic Economy, 1860–1914.* Toronto: McClelland & Stewart, 1991.

Rogers, E.S., and D.B. Smith, eds. *Aboriginal Ontario: Historical*

Perspectives on the First Nations. Toronto: Ontario Historical
Studies Series, 1994.

Sturino, F. 'The Role of Women in Italian Immigration to the
New World.' In *Looking Through My Sister's Eyes: An Exploration
in Women's History,* ed. J. Burnet. Toronto: Multicultural
History Society of Ontario, 1986.

Van Kirk, S. *'Many Tender Ties': Women in Fur-Trade Society in
Western Canada, 1670–1870.* Winnipeg: Watson & Dwyer, 1980.

Ward, P. *Courtship, Love and Marriage in Nineteenth-Century English
Canada.* Montreal and Kingston: McGill-Queen's University
Press, 1990.

Westfall, W. *Two Worlds: The Protestant Culture of Nineteenth-Century
Ontario.* Montreal and Kingston: McGill-Queen's University
Press, 1989.

Yee, S. 'Gender Ideology and Black Women as Community
Builders in Ontario, 1850–70.' *Canadian Historical Review* 75/1
(March 1994): 53–73.

Chapter 2: Mending Crisis-Torn Families

Allen, R. *The Social Passion: Religion and Social Reform in Canada.*
Toronto: University of Toronto Press, 1971.

Arnup, K., A. Lévesque, and R. Roach Pierson, eds. *Delivering
Motherhood: Maternal Ideologies and Practices in the Nineteenth and
Twentieth Centuries.* London: Routledge, 1990.

Baillargeon, D. 'Fréquenter les Gouttes de lait: L'experience des
mères montréalaises, 1910–1965.' *Revue d'histoire de l'Amérique
française* 50/1 (Summer 1996): 29–68.

Benoit, C. *Midwives in Passage.* St John's, Newf.: Institute for
Social and Economic Research, 1991.

Bliss, M. 'Pure Books on Avoided Subjects: Pre-Freudian Sexual
Ideas in Canada.' In *Medicine in Canadian Society: Historical
Perspectives,* ed. S.E.D. Shortt. Montreal and Kingston: McGill-
Queen's University Press, 1982.

Burke, S. *Seeking the Highest Good: Social Service and Gender at the
University of Toronto, 1888–1937.* Toronto: University of Toronto Press, 1995.

Cavanaugh, C., and R.R. Warne, eds. *Standing on New Ground: Women in Alberta*. Edmonton: University of Alberta Press, 1993.

Copp, T. *The Anatomy of Poverty: The Condition of the Working Class in Montreal*. Toronto: McClelland & Stewart, 1974.

Cook, R., and R.C. Brown. *Canada, 1896–1921: A Nation Transformed*. Toronto: McClelland & Stewart, 1974.

Cook, S.A. *Through Sunshine and Shadow: The Woman's Christian Temperance Union, Evangelicalism and Reform in Ontario, 1874–1930*. Montreal and Kingston: McGill-Queen's University Press, 1995.

Fingard, J. *The Dark Side of Life in Victorian Halifax*. Porters Lake, N.S.: Pottersfield, 1989.

– 'The Prevention of Cruelty, Marriage Breakdown and the Rights of Wives in Nova Scotia, 1880–1900.' *Acadiensis* 22/2 (Spring 1993): 84–101.

Harvey, K. 'Amazons and Victims: Resisting Wife Abuse in Working-Class Montreal, 1869–1879.' In *Journal of the Canadian Historical Association* 2 (1991): 131–48.

Houston, S. 'The Waifs and Strays of a Victorian City: Juvenile Delinquents in Toronto.' In *Childhood and Family in Canadian History*, ed. J. Parr. Toronto: McClelland & Stewart, 1983.

Kinsman, G. *The Regulation of Desire: Sexuality in Canada*. Montreal: Black Rose, 1987.

McLaren, A. *Our Own Master Race: Eugenics in Canada*. Toronto: McClelland & Stewart, 1990.

Miller, J.R. *Shingwauk's Vision: A History of Native Residential Schools*. Toronto: University of Toronto Press, 1996.

Noel, Jan. *Canada Dry: Temperance Crusades before Confederation*. Toronto: University of Toronto Press, 1995.

Piva, M. *The Condition of the Working Class in Toronto*. Ottawa: University of Ottawa Press, 1979.

Purdy, S. '"This Is Not a Company; It Is a Cause": Class, Gender and the Toronto Housing Company.' *Urban History Review* 21/2 (March 1993): 75–91.

Rooke, P., and R.L. Schnell. *Discarding the Asylum: From Child Welfare to the Welfare State in English Canada*. Lanham, Md.: University Press of America, 1983.

Snell, J. *In the Shadow of the Law: Divorce in Canada, 1900–1939.*
Toronto: University of Toronto Press, 1991.
Snell, J. *The Citizen's Wage: The State and the Elderly in Canada,
1900-1951.* Toronto: University of Toronto Press, 1995.
Strange, C. *Toronto's Girl Problem: The Perils and Pleasures of the
City, 1880–1930.* Toronto: University of Toronto Press, 1995.
Strange, C., and T. Loo. *Making Good: Law and Moral Regulation
in Canada, 1867–1939.* Toronto: University of Toronto Press,
1997.
Sutherland, N. *Children in English-Canadian Society: Framing the
Twentieth-Century Consensus.* Toronto: University of Toronto
Press, 1976.
Ursel, J. *Private Lives, Public Policy: 100 Years of State Intervention in
the Family.* Toronto: Women's Press, 1992.
Valverde, M. *The Age of Light, Soap and Water: Moral Reform in
English Canada, 1885–1925.* Toronto: McClelland & Stewart,
1991.

Chapter 3: War and Reconstruction

Brody, H. *The People's Land: Inuit, Whites and the Eastern Arctic,* 2d
ed. Vancouver: Douglas & MacIntyre, 1991.
Bourne, P., W. Mitchinson, P. Bristow, G. Cuthbert Brandt,
B. Light, N. Black, and A. Prentice. *Canadian Women: A History,*
2d ed. Toronto: Harcourt, Brace, Jovanovich, 1995.
Burnet, J., and H. Palmer. *'Coming Canadians': An Introduction to
a History of Canada's Peoples.* Toronto: McClelland & Stewart,
1988.
Cook, R., and R. Brown. *Canada, 1896–1921: A Nation Trans-
formed.* Toronto: McClelland & Stewart, 1974.
Dubinsky, K. *Improper Advances: Rape and Heterosexual Conflict in
Ontario, 1880–1929.* Chicago: University of Chicago Press, 1993.
Guest, D. *The Emergence of Social Security in Canada.* Vancouver:
University of British Columbia Press, 1985.
Kalman, H. *A History of Canadian Architecture,* vol. 2. Don Mills,
Ont.: Oxford University Press, 1995.
Lévesque, A. *La Norme et les déviantes: Des femmes au Québec pendant
l'entre-deux-guerres.* Montreal: Rémue-Ménage, 1989; trans. by

Y. Klein as *Making and Breaking the Rules: Women in Quebec, 1919–1939*. Toronto: McClelland & Stewart, 1994.

Lewis, N., ed. *'I Want to Join Your Club': Letters from Rural Children, 1900–1920*. Waterloo, Ont.: Wilfrid Laurier University Press, 1996.

Miller, J.R. *Shingwauk's Vision: A History of Native Residential Schools*. Toronto: University of Toronto Press, 1996.

Morton, S. *Ideal Surroundings: Domestic Life in a Halifax Working-Class Suburb in the 1920s*. Toronto: University of Toronto Press, 1995.

Palmer, B.D. *Working Class Experience*, 2d ed. Toronto: McClelland & Stewart, 1992.

Petroff, L. *Sojourners and Settlers: The Macedonian Community in Toronto to 1940*. Toronto: Multicultural History Society of Ontario, 1995.

Read, D. ed. *The Great War and Canadian Society: An Oral History*. Toronto: Hogtown Press, 1978.

Rogers, E.S., and D.B. Smith, eds. *Aboriginal Ontario: Historical Perspectives on the First Nations*. Toronto: Ontario Historical Studies Series, 1994.

Shore, M. *The Science of Social Redemption: McGill, the Chicago School, and the Origins of Social Research in Canada*. Toronto: University of Toronto Press, 1987.

Snell, J. *In the Shadow of the Law: Divorce in Canada, 1900–1939*. Toronto: University of Toronto Press, 1991.

Snell, J. *The Citizen's Wage: The State and the Elderly in Canada, 1900–1951*. Toronto: University of Toronto Press, 1995.

Strong-Boag, V. *The New Day Recalled: Lives of Girls and Women in English Canada, 1919–1939*. Toronto: Penguin, 1988.

Swyripa, F. *Wedded to the Cause: Ukrainian-Canadian Women and Ethnic Identity, 1891–1991*. Toronto: University of Toronto Press, 1993.

Taylor, J. *Fashioning Farmers: Ideology, Agricultural Knowledge and the Manitoba Farm Movement, 1890–1925*. Regina: Canadian Plains Research Center, 1994.

Thompson, J.H. *The Harvests of War*. Toronto: McClelland & Stewart, 1978.

Thompson, J.H., and A. Seager. *Canada, 1922–39: Decades of Discord*. Toronto: McClelland & Stewart, 1985.

Ursel, J. *Private Lives, Public Policy: 100 Years of State Intervention in the Family.* Toronto: Women's Press, 1992.

Valverde, M. *The Age of Light, Soap and Water: Moral Reform in English Canada, 1885–1925.* Toronto: McClelland & Stewart, 1991.

Chapter 4: New Model Families

Arnup, K. *Education for Motherhood: Advice for Mothers in Twentieth-Century Canada.* Toronto: University of Toronto Press, 1994.

Chunn, D. *From Punishment to Doing Good: Family Courts and Socialized Justice in Ontario, 1880–1940.* Toronto: University of Toronto Press, 1992.

Comacchio, C.R. *'Nations Are Built of Babies': Saving Ontario's Mothers and Children, 1900–1940.* Montreal and Kingston: McGill-Queen's University Press, 1993.

Coulter, R. 'The Working Young of Edmonton, 1921–31.' In *Childhood and Family in Canadian History,* ed. J. Parr. Toronto: McClelland & Stewart, 1983.

Lévesque, A. *La Norme et les déviantes: Des femmes au Québec pendant l'entre-deux-guerres.* Montreal: Rémue-Ménage, 1989; trans. by Y. Klein as *Making and Breaking the Rules: Women in Quebec, 1919–1939.* Toronto: McClelland & Stewart, 1994.

Little, M.J.H. *'No Car, No Radio, No Liquor Permit': The Moral Regulation of Single Mothers in Ontario, 1920–1997.* Toronto: Oxford University Press, 1998.

McLaren, A. *Our Own Master Race: Eugenics in Canada.* Toronto: McClelland & Stewart, 1990.

McLaren, A., and A.T. McLaren. *The Bedroom and the State: The Changing Practices and Politics of Contraception and Abortion in Canada.* Toronto: McClelland & Stewart, 1986.

Parr, J. *The Gender of Breadwinners: Women, Men and Change in Two Industrial Towns, 1880–1950.* Toronto: University of Toronto Press, 1990.

Rosenfeld, M. '"It Was a Hard Life": Class and Gender in the Work and Family Rhythms of a Railway Town, 1920–50.' In *Canadian Family History: Selected Readings,* ed. B. Bradbury. Toronto: Copp Clark Pitman, 1992.

Shore, M. *The Science of Social Redemption: McGill, the Chicago School, and the Origins of Social Research in Canada.* Toronto: University of Toronto Press, 1987.

Strong-Boag, V. *The New Day Recalled: Lives of Girls and Women in English Canada, 1919–1939.* Toronto: Penguin, 1988.

Struthers, J. *The Limits of Affluence: Welfare in Ontario, 1920–1970.* Toronto: Ontario Historical Studies Series, 1994.

Taylor, J. *Fashioning Farmers: Ideology, Agricultural Knowledge and the Manitoba Farm Movement, 1890–1925.* Regina: Canadian Plains Research Center, 1994.

Waldram, J.B., D.A. Herring, and T.K. Young. *Aboriginal Health in Canada: Historical, Cultural, and Epidemiological Perspectives.* Toronto: University of Toronto Press, 1995.

Chapter 5: Families in Distress

Arnup, K. *Education for Motherhood.* Toronto: University of Toronto Press, 1994.

Axelrod, P. *Making a Middle Class: Student Life in English Canada During the Thirties.* Montreal and Kingston: McGill-Queen's University Press, 1990.

Baillargeon, Denyse. *Ménagères au temps de la Crise.* Montreal: Rémue-Ménage, 1991.

Berton, P. *The Great Depression.* Toronto: McClelland & Stewart, 1990.

Bliss, M., and L.M. Grayson, eds. *The Wretched of Canada: Letters to R.B. Bennett.* Toronto: University of Toronto Press, 1971.

Bourne, P., W. Mitchinson, P. Bristow, G. Cuthbert Brandt, B. Light, N. Black, and A. Prentice. *Canadian Women: A History,* 2d ed. Toronto: Harcourt, Brace, Jovanovich, 1995.

Broadfoot, B. *Ten Lost Years, 1929–39: Memories of Canadians Who Survived the Depression.* Toronto: Doubleday, 1973.

Chong, D. *The Concubine's Children.* Toronto: Penguin, 1994.

Chunn, D. *From Punishment to Doing Good: Family Courts and Socialized Justice in Ontario, 1880–1940.* Toronto: University of Toronto Press, 1992.

Comacchio, C.R. *'Nations Are Built of Babies': Saving Ontario's Mothers and Children, 1900–1940.* Montreal and Kingston: McGill-Queen's University Press, 1993.

Dodd, D. 'The Canadian Birth Control Movement on Trial.'
   Histoire sociale/Social History 16/32 (November 1983): 411–28.
– 'The Hamilton Birth Control Clinic of the 1930s.' *Ontario
   History* 75/1 (March 1993): 71–86.
Emery, G. *Facts of Life: The Social Construction of Vital Statistics,
   Ontario, 1869–1952.* Montreal and Kingston: McGill-Queen's
   University Press, 1993.
Finkel, A. 'Origins of the Welfare State in Canada.' In *Interpreting
   Canada's Past*, vol. 2, ed. J. Bumsted. Toronto: Oxford Univer-
   sity Press, 1993.
Forbes, E.R. *Challenging the Regional Stereotype: Essays on the
   Twentieth-Century Maritimes.* Fredericton, N.B.: Acadiensis,
   1989.
Gray, J. *The Winter Years.* Toronto: Macmillan, 1966.
Guest, D. 'World War II and the Welfare State in Canada.' In *The
   Benevolent State: The Growth of Welfare in Canada*, ed. A. Mosco-
   vitch and J. Albert. Toronto: Garamond, 1987.
Hobbs, M. 'Equality and Difference: Feminism and the Defense
   of Women Workers During the Great Depression.' *Labour/Le
   Travail* 32 (Fall 1993): 201–23.
Horn, M. ed. *The Dirty Thirties: Canadians in the Great Depression.*
   Toronto: Copp Clark, 1972.
Johnston, W. 'Keeping Children in School: The Response of the
   Montreal Roman Catholic School Commission to the Depres-
   sion of the 1930s.' In Canadian Historical Association, *Histori-
   cal Papers*, 1985.
Luxton, M. *More Than a Labour of Love: Three Generations of
   Women's Work in the Home.* Toronto: Women's Press, 1980.
McLaren, A., and A.T. McLaren. *The Bedroom and the State: The
   Changing Practices and Politics of Contraception and Abortion in
   Canada.* Toronto: McClelland & Stewart, 1986.
Morrison, R.B., and C.R. Wilson, eds. *Native Peoples: The Cana-
   dian Experience,* 2d ed. Toronto: McClelland & Stewart, 1995.
Pierson, R.R. 'Gender and the Unemployment Insurance
   Debates in Canada, 1934–40.' *Labour/Le Travail* 25 (Spring
   1990): 77–103.
Richardson, T. *The Century of the Child: The Mental Hygiene*

Movement and Social Policy in the United States and Canada. New York: State University of New York Press, 1989.

Roberts, B. *Whence They Came: Deportation from Canada, 1900–1935*. Ottawa: University of Ottawa Press, 1988.

Sager, E. *Ships and Memories: Merchant Seafarers in Canada's Age of Steam*. Vancouver: UBC Press, 1993.

Shore, M. *The Science of Social Redemption: McGill, the Chicago School, and the Origins of Social Research in Canada*. Toronto: University of Toronto Press, 1987.

Snell, J. *The Citizen's Wage: The State and the Elderly in Canada, 1900–1951*. Toronto: University of Toronto Press, 1995.

Strong-Boag, V. *The New Day Recalled: Lives of Girls and Women in English Canada, 1919–1939*. Toronto: Penguin, 1988.

Struthers, J. *No Fault of Their Own*. Toronto: University of Toronto Press, 1983.

Struthers, J. *The Limits of Affluence: Welfare in Ontario, 1920–1970*. Toronto: Ontario Historical Studies Series, 1994.

Taylor, J.H. 'Sources of Political Conflict in the Thirties: Welfare Policy and the Geography of Need.' In *The Benevolent State*, ed. Moscovitch and Albert.

Thompson, J.H., and A. Seager. *Canada, 1922–1939: Decades of Discord*. Toronto: McClelland & Stewart, 1985.

Valverde, M. 'Families, Private Property, and the State: The Dionnes and the Toronto Stork Derby.' *Journal of Canadian Studies* 29/4 (Winter 1994–5): 15–35.

Waldram, J.B., D.A. Herring, and T.K. Young. *Aboriginal Health in Canada: Historical, Cultural and Epidemiological Perspectives*. Toronto: University of Toronto Press, 1995.

Index

Aberhart, William, 144–5
Aboriginal peoples, 3, 7, 10,
    15–18, 20–2, 24–5, 28–30,
    32, 36, 43, 45–6, 52, 54–5,
    57, 67, 70–1, 84–5, 94–5,
    116, 118–19, 121, 123, 127,
    129, 151–2, 154; and re-
    serves, 10, 30, 45–6, 52, 54,
    71, 84, 94–5, 121, 129, 151;
    and residential schools,
    54–5, 84–5, 94–5; *see also*
    Indian Act; Indian Affairs;
    Inuit; Métis
abortion, 59, 101, 133; *see also*
    birth control; family limita-
    tion
adolescence, 8, 10, 15, 18,
    24–5, 47, 53, 74, 86–8,
    99–100, 103, 116, 147; *see*
    also youth
adoption, 18, 106
adulthood, 8, 24, 30–1, 105,
    138, 147, 152
advice (literature), 59–60,
    95–9, 103, 108, 132–3, 136–7

African Canadians, 7, 10, 19,
    29, 35, 118–19, 125–6
agriculture. *See* rural families
Alberta, 58, 87, 104, 113, 131,
    144
alcohol, 20, 37, 40, 49, 58, 69,
    70, 84, 91–2; prohibition,
    69, 91–2; Woman's Chris-
    tian Temperance Union,
    49, 58, 70, 91–2
anti-Communism, 118, 132,
    139, 140

Bennett, R.B., 115, 120;
    Bennett New Deal [1935],
    144; Bennett Relief Act
    [1930], 115; *see also* Great
    Depression; relief; state;
    social welfare
birth control, 10, 27, 58, 88,
    98, 101–2, 108, 130–3; Birth
    Control Society of Canada
    [1931], 132; Canadian Birth
    Control League [1924],
    101; Eastview Trial, 132–3;

nutrition, 119–21, 125–9,
147; malnutrition, 120–1;
minimum/maximum
standards, 145–7

Ontario, 19, 25, 29, 32–4, 37,
43, 49, 53, 55, 70, 73, 84, 86,
92, 100, 104–5, 116, 119,
121, 129–30, 132, 142
orphans, 18, 22, 29, 33, 55,
65, 106, 108

Palmer, Dorothea, 132–3; *see
also* birth control
parenting, 19, 22, 30–1, 38,
42–3, 51, 54–7, 77, 85, 95–6,
105, 108, 133–6, 144, 152,
153–4; *see also* fatherhood;
childrearing; motherhood
Parents' Information Bureau
[1930], 132–3; *see also* birth
control
patriarchy, 5, 9, 19, 21, 38, 42,
43, 46, 60, 66, 88–9, 91, 104,
108, 117, 125, 135, 142,
151–4; *see also* domesticity;
gender; family ideals; fatherhood; state; women
poverty, 29–30, 34, 46, 51–2,
58, 72, 77, 87, 98, 107,
113–14, 117–29; 131–2, 135,
140, 142–8; *see also* family
economy; family strategies;
relief; social welfare; state;
unemployment
Prince Edward Island, 25, 116,
140, 143

production. *See* domestic
production; industry
provinces/regions. *See individual entries*
psychology, 97, 135–7, 153–4;
Dr William Blatz, 97, 136–7;
Dr G. Stanley Hall, 56; Dr
John B. Watson, 97; *see also*
advice (literature); childrearing; experts; manage-
ment; medicine
punctuated equilibrium, 5,
15, 65–6, 114, 149

Quebec, 6, 22–3, 25, 27, 29,
32, 34–5, 37, 39, 49, 51–3,
61, 69–71, 73, 83, 86, 92–3,
98, 100–1, 113, 115, 121,
124, 130, 142

race, racism, 5, 9, 19, 21 40,
42, 45–6, 49, 51–2, 54, 59,
66, 71, 73, 91, 93–4, 98–9,
101, 116, 118, 131, 151;
race suicide, 73, 91, 101; *see
also* degeneration; eugenics
recreation, 74–5, 80–1, 85–7,
97–100, 106, 119, 122,
129–30, 138–9, 140
reform, 15, 27, 41, 48, 49–54,
56, 58–9, 60–2, 67, 88–91,
94, 100, 106–7, 147, 153–4;
see also Moral and Social
Reform Council; Social
Gospel; social welfare
religion, 5, 15–16, 36, 42, 48,
54, 58, 60, 84–5, 101, 133;

THEMES IN CANADIAN HISTORY

Editors:
Colin Coates 2003–
Craig Heron 1997–
Franca Iacovetta 1997–1999